THE

SIEGE OF SAVANNAH

BY

COUNT D'ESTAING.

1779.

Eyewitness Accounts of the American Revolution

The Siege of Savannah
by the Fleet of
Count D'Estaing in 1779

Edited by

Charles C. Jones, Jr.

The New York Times & Arno Press

THE

SIEGE OF SAVANNAH,

IN

1779,

AS DESCRIBED IN TWO CONTEMPORANEOUS JOURNALS
OF FRENCH OFFICERS

IN

THE FLEET OF COUNT D'ESTAING.

———•—————

ALBANY, N. Y.:
JOEL MUNSELL, 82 STATE STREET.
1874.

Very truly yours,
Charles C. Jones Jr.

TO THE

GEORGIA HISTORICAL SOCIETY,

THIS

CONTRIBUTION TO THE HISTORY

OF THE

SIEGE OF SAVANNAH IN 1779

IS

CORDIALLY DEDICATED.

INTRODUCTION.

To the kindness of Mr. J. Carson Brevoort, of Brooklyn, am I indebted for the loan both of the French manuscript from which the following translation has been prepared, and of the autograph map here reproduced. The former, beautifully written in a delicate, regular hand, is evidently a copy, by a professional scribe, of the journal of some French officer present at the siege of Savannah and during the movements of D'Estaing's fleet antecedent to and consequent upon that memorable occurrence.

It is clear, from its internal evidence, that the original was a contemporaneous document. The present tense is used in nearly every instance; and the probabilities are that it was penned day by day as the events, of which it treats, transpired. The forms of expression, words, and the construction of the sentences are such as were current among French writers about a century ago.

While an adept with his pen, the scribe was, not infrequently, negligent in preserving the proper accents and capital letters, and unmindful of suitable punctuation. He is also occasionally at fault in his spelling. The labor of the translator was thus rendered somewhat tedious, but in the end not uncertain. To my friend Prof. Charles Rau of New York city, special acknowledgments are due for most valuable assistance. Unfortunately the name of the author of this Journal has not been preserved. Without doubt, however, he was personally cognizant of the movements of which he speaks, and an actor in the scenes here described.

From English and American sources we derive extended accounts of the siege of Savannah, but the accompanying Journal furnishes us with the most satisfactory French narrative of which we have any knowledge. An interior view is here presented of the intentions and operations of D'Estaing, and of the disposition and labors of his army, which appears nowhere else with the same minuteness of detail, and accuracy of description.   Despite the fact that the coöperation of the American forces under General Lincoln is recognized by little more than a bare mention of their presence and partial participation in the assault, and although undue prominence be given to the actions of the French, this account happily supplements the narratives already before the public, and forms a most valuable contribution to the history of the siege.

We have taken the liberty of adding notes where they appeared conducive to a fuller appreciation of the events alluded to.

The original map (of which we have here a reproduction by the photolithographic process), was purchased in London at the late sale of Lord Rawdon's papers, and was selected from his military portfolio. While its general resemblance to the map of the siege of Savannah contained in "Faden's Plans of Battles in North America" will be readily conceded, we think the present map more elaborate and satisfactory in its details.   It is apparently the work of a German or Swiss engineer who may have been connected with either Wissenbach's or Trumbach's Hessian regiment, both of which were present at the siege and constituted a part of the English garrison.   By an endorsement it seems at one time to have been the property of Lieutenant Finnegan of the Sixteenth regiment of Infantry.   Two companies of that regiment held the entrenchments to the left of the Augusta road, and rendered efficient service in the repulse of the assault of the 9th of October.

As furnishing another French account of the siege, and as illustrating the opinion entertained by at least one officer in D'Estaing's fleet of the expediency and conduct of this demonstration against Savannah, we have translated and appended some extracts from the Journal of a naval officer who participated in the expedition.   This Journal was printed in Paris in 1782.   The privations endured and the dangers encountered by the French fleet while upon the Georgia coast are vividly portrayed.   It is interesting also to note the estimate here formed of Count D'Estaing as a man and as a commander.

Both the manuscript and the printed Journal were procured in Paris, at the Luzarche sale, on the first of March, 1869.

CHARLES C. JONES, JR.

NEW YORK,
June 1st, 1874.

THE

SIEGE OF SAVANNAH,

BY

COUNT D'ESTAING.

1779.

SIEGE OF SAVANNAH.

1779.

July 19th. | *Monday*, at four o'clock in the morning, M. D'Estaing makes his appearance in the roadstead of Basse Terre.

idem. | At three o'clock P.M. three hundred and fifty men from the regiment of Armagnac, an equal number from the regiment of Guadeloupe, and thirty-one artillerymen are taken on board the fleet.

20th. | *Tuesday* morning preparation is made for sailing.

21st. | *Wednesday* morning Count D'Estaing orders the ships *Le Robuste* and *L'Annibal*, and the frigates *Iphigenie* and *La Chimere* to detach themselves from the fleet, and, proceeding to the leeward, to take a position before the forts of Montserrat.

Towards noon *La Chimere*, which was in the advance, encountered twenty-five or thirty cannon shots from the batteries without, however, sustaining any injury from them. The Hannibal, commanded by M. de la Motte-piquet;[1] is also cannonaded. Having replied with one hundred discharges from his twenty-four and thirty-six pounder guns, directed against the city and the batteries, this officer joins M. De Grasse, commanding *Le Robuste*, who was standing to his leeward.

[1] Spelled in the manuscript *Mothepiquet*.

1779. Near four o'clock P.M. the frigate Lively conveys to the two ships, and the two frigates, an order to return to the squadron; which they join before nightfall.

July
22nd.
Thursday morning, about ten o'clock, the French squadron defiles in order of battle before the English squadron which was lying in the roadstead of St. Christopher, with broad-sides brought to bear upon the French. The English squadron was composed of twenty vessels, three of which had lost their top-masts in the battle at Grenada.[1]

Resolved by a countermarch at long range cannon shot to pass a second time nearer the English, Count De Grasse, whom Count D'Estaing had charged with attacking the enemy if he deemed the matter practicable, conducts the movement.[2]

23rd.
Friday, Count D'Estaing dispatches to Basse Terre some frigates to bring the merchant fleet, to which that of Martinique had been united, and to conduct it to the squadron which, before St. Christopher and Montserrat, waited to convoy it.

26th.
On *Monday* the merchant fleet joined the squadron which sailed for St. Domingo.

31st.
Saturday, at four o'clock in the afternoon, the squadron arrived in the harbor of the Cape.[3] In entering, the Amphion touched bottom and lost her rudder. Some of the other vessels were damaged. Upon landing we are informed of the declaration of war by Spain.

Aug.
Tuesday. Count D'Estaing comes on board the Chimere, and, with the ships *Artesien*, *Fendant*, and *Sagittaire*, the frigates *Minerve* and *Chimere*, and one cutter, sails for the mole of St. Nicholas.

[1] Count D'Estaing, early in this month, had reduced this place in gallant style, after a sharp action.

[2] This offer of battle was declined by the English.

[3] François.

1779.   *Wednesday.* D'Estaing goes ashore at the mole, from which he returns
⌣   by land some days afterwards.
Aug.4.

7th.   *Saturday.* Arrival at Port au Prince of the division of the *Fendant,*
commanded by M. de Vaudreuil, and embarkation of the troops.

10th.   Fête given at the Cape,[1] on board the *Languedoc,* by Count D'Estaing,
in celebration of the alliance with Spain.

11th.   *Wednesday.* Removal of the troops from the Wind-ward islands and
their location in ships and frigates other than those in which they had
been embarked for the Cape.

13th.   *Friday.* M. de Vaudreuil's division leaves Port au Prince for the
mole of St. Nicholas, where it arrives on the 26th,[2] and receives troops
on board.

16th.   *Monday.* Count D'Estaing sails from the Cape with the fleet, and a
convoy from the Wind-ward islands and St. Domingo composed of sixty
sails.[3]   During this voyage of the 17th and 18th the squadron keeps
to the windward, and is joined by the division of M. de Vaudreuil which
left the mole on the 17th.

18th.   *Wednesday.* Passed near Tortugas.

19th.   *Thursday.* Came in sight of Great Inagua, a low and uninhabited
island.

20th.   *Friday.* Sighted and passed to the leeward of Miraporvos and the
Fortune islands, a cluster of low lying islands, and like Inagua, uninhabited.   In the afternoon of the same day we observed Crooked island.

---

[1] François.

[2] Should be the 16*th ;* see postea.

[3] Marshall, in his *Life of Washington,* [vol. IV, p. 95. Philadelphia, 1805] computes
the strength of the land army on board the fleet, at six thousand men.

1779.   *Saturday.* The General took advantage of a calm to hoist the commander's flag.   An officer from each vessel repaired on board the ship
Aug.   Languedoc and received particular instructions and signals for landing.
21st.   Sealed orders relating to the debarkation, addressed to the commanders
of the troops on the respective vessels, were furnished by the Major
General of the land army.

22nd.   On *Sunday* and *Monday* we sailed in sight of the Watling islands
and   which, in all respects, resembled the islands we had noticed on pre-
23rd.   vious days.

At three o'clock P.M. on *Sunday*, the merchant convoy separates
itself from the squadron and is escorted by the *Protecteur* and the *Fier*,
and by the frigates *Minerve, Alcméne* and *Aimable.*

At the time of its departure from the Windward islands the fleet was
composed of twenty-five ships — including the *Fier Rodrigue* — thirteen
frigates, and one cutter.   The *Amphion* was absent, having remained
at the Cape.   After our separation from the convoy, the fleet was reduced
to twenty-two ships of the line, ten frigates, and one cutter.   There
were also several barges and transport schooners, and some American
vessels.

Sept.   *Wednesday,* at seven o'clock P.M. we anchored in fifteen fathoms
1st.   water, fourteen or fifteen leagues east of the coast of Georgia, and in
the thirty-first degree of north latitude.

2nd.   *Thursday.* The sea very rough.   The winds veering from east to
south compelled a part of the squadron, which had lost both cables
and anchors, to put to sea.

4th.   *Saturday.* South-east winds have restored a calm, and the fleet is
again united.

7th.   *Tuesday.* The squadron gets under way to approach the land.

1779.
Sept.
8th.

Wednesday. We cast anchor four leagues in front of Tybee[1] island.

A division composed of the *Artesien*, the *Fantasque*, the *Chimére*, the *Blanche*, the *Fortunée* and the *Iphigenie* is detached from the fleet to advance and come to anchor at the distance of a league and a half from Tybee.

9th.

Count D'Estaing directs the embarkation of seven hundred troops in the long boats, to await his further orders. The General himself goes on board the *Chimére* and, with three other frigates, prepares to force a passage across the bar of the Savannah[2] river. He had scarcely gotten under way when the galleys or frigates of the enemy, which were lying at anchor near the mouth of the river, moved a league higher up.[3] At the same time the English opened fire upon us from Fort Tybee.[4] Our four frigates came to anchor above the bar, having crossed it without encountering any obstacle. At nightfall Count D'Estaing orders the disembarkation of the troops on board the frigates, and directs the long boats[5] to be brought along aside of the *Chimére* that they might move in concert.

As the general's cutter, in which there was a detachment of only fifteen men, belonging to the regiment of Armagnac, moved much faster than the long boats, the General, being unwilling to wait for them, landed himself on Tybee island which he found evacuated by the enemy. Having visited the environs of the fort, he posts two sentinels and goes quietly to sleep. The long boats were unable to compass a landing until two hours afterwards. From these boats two hundred men of different regiments were put on shore.

[1] Spelled in the manuscript, *Tiby.*

[2] In the manuscript written *Savanah.*

[3] The English vessels alluded to were the ships *Rose*, *Fowey*, *Kepple* and *Germain*, the *Comet*, a galley, and several small craft. Upon the approach of the French they weighed anchor and retired to Five-fathom hole.

[4] Fort Tybee, located near the light house on the northern extremity of Great Tybee island, was designed to guard the entrance into Savannah river. At this time it was feebly garrisoned. It's armament consisted of one twenty-four pounder gun and an eight and a half inch howitzer.

[5] Already filled with seven hundred men.

1779.   *Friday*, at day-break, the General orders the *Iphigenie* to reëmbark
⏜   her troops and join the squadron.   He himself returns to his ship and
Sept.   thence causes all the landing troops of the fleet from the ships the Han-
10th.   nibal, the Guerrier, the Sphinx, the Vengeur, the Artesien and the
          Provence, to pass in review before him.   At ten o'clock at night the
          troops which were on Tybee island were taken on board the two frigates
          La Blanche and *La Fortunée*.   Only twenty-five men of the regiment
          of Armagnac were left on board the Chimére.

11th.   *Saturday*. The six ships above named, with all the long boats of the
          squadron and the cutters, weighed anchors and the same day dropped
          them again six leagues to the south, and at a distance of four leagues
          from the mouth of Ossaba river, at which point a disembarkation had
          been determined upon.[1]   Twelve hundred men from different regiments
          were placed in the long boats and cutters.

12th.   *Sunday*. At nine o'clock at night these troops set foot on land at
          Beaulieu,[2] situated four leagues from the mouth of the Ossaba river,
          and six leagues to the south of Savannah.   This point[3] was guarded
          by thirty men who evacuated it upon the approach of our troops, whose
          landing was in no manner hindered.

[1] The Viscount de Fontanges, Adjutant-General of the army, who, in the frigate Amazon, commanded by the famous navigator La Perouse, had been dispatched by Count
D'Estaing to confer with General Lincoln, arrived in Charleston, South Carolina, on the
4th of September.   A concert of action between the French fleet and the Americans, for
the reduction of Savannah, was quickly agreed upon.   Boats were sent from Charleston
to assist in landing troops, ordnance, and stores.   Colonel Cambray of the Engineers,
Colonel Thomas Pinckney, Aid to General Lincoln, and Captain Gadsden were detailed
to return with the Viscount and assist Count D'Estaing in consummating his landing
upon the Georgia coast.

At Ossaba, Count D'Estaing was met by Colonel Joseph Habersham who had proceeded
thither to indicate the proper place for and to facilitate the debarkation of the troops.

[2] Written *Bwly* in the manuscript.

[3] Colonel Pinckney states that the British force stationed at this point, with two field
pieces, had been withdrawn the preceding day.   Had any resistance been offered, the
French, in open boats and unsupported by the fleet, would necessarily have been subjected
to considerable loss.

1779.   Information is received of the capture of the frigate Ariel[1] by the
Amazon, commanded by M de la Perouze, a lieutenant of the navy.
Sept. 12th.   M. Roger, a captain of the regiment of Guadeloupe, was ordered by the
General to occupy a position distant three leagues from Beaulieu in the
direction of Savannah, and along the line of Ossaba river.   Here he
captured two barges and some long boats freighted with articles and
merchandise, and ten prisoners.   He reports his achievement to the
General, and also communicates the fact that intelligence had just reached
him that he would be immediately attacked by two hundred men.
This determined Count D'Estaing to dispatch, at once, M. Odune, with
three hundred men, for the relief of M. Roger.

idem.   General Pulaski,[2] with some officers of his command, comes to wel-
come M. D'Estaing.

[1] This capture was made on the 11th, after a gallant resistance offered on the part of
the English commander.   The *Amazon* carried a battery of thirty-six guns, while the
Ariel had only twenty-four.

[2] Spelled *Polasky* in the manuscript.

Pulaski, who, after Prevost's retreat from South Carolina, had taken post on a ridge
fifty miles north-east of Augusta for the convenience of obtaining provisions and to be
within easy march of either Augusta or Charleston as occasion might require, was ordered
to join General McIntosh at Augusta.   With this united command General McIntosh
was directed to move toward Savannah in advance of the army under General Lincoln
which was coming from Charleston, attack the British outposts, and open communi-
cation with the French troops upon the coast.   Pressing forward, General McIntosh took
a position between Savannah and Great Ogeechee ferry.   Count Pulaski cut off one of
the enemy's pickets, killing and wounding five men and capturing a subaltern and five
privates.   Several skirmishes were had with the British outposts before he joined the
French at Beaulieu.   As soon as Count D'Estaing had effected a landing, General McIntosh
returned and halted at Millen's plantation, where he awaited the arrival of General
Lincoln.

See M'Call's History of Georgia, vol. II, p. 247.   Captain Bentalou (*Reply to Judge
Johnson's Remarks* etc., p. 33.   Baltimore, 1826) asserts that Count D'Estaing informed
Pulaski, upon their meeting at Beaulieu, that he intended to march at once upon Savannah
without waiting for General Lincoln, and that " he counted on his Legion to form his
van."   " In pursuance of this wish," continues Captain Bentalou, " we set out immediately
and reached Savannah sometime before D'Estaing, where we engaged and cut off an advanced picket of the enemy's infantry."

1779.   The armed store ships *La Bricole* and *La Truite*, carrying eighteen
and twelve pounder guns, enter the **Savannah** river to join the *Chimére*
Sept.   under the command of M. **Durumain, who** exchanges a cannonade with
12th.   the English galleys without injury to either side.

13th.   The frigates *La Fortunée* and *La Blanche* leave Savannah river to
receive the orders which M. D'Estaing had left for them with M. de
Broves commanding the remainder of the fleet.   They come to anchor
near the *Cæsar*, at ten o'clock in the morning.   At noon they are ordered to disembark their troops at Ossaba river.   The rough weather
did not permit them to raise their anchors, and the wind, which had
suddenly increased to a gale, compelled them to slip their cables.   The
same thing happened to the squadron of M. de Broves who, in like
manner, abandoned his anchors.   The violence of the wind did not
suffer the fleet to return to its anchorage before the 20th.   Several
vessels were severely injured, and the ship *La Blanche* was at one time
on the eve of cutting away her mizzen-mast.

idem.   Two American galleys, armed with eighteen and twenty-four pounder
guns and coming from Charles-Town, proceeded to join M. Durumain.

15th.   *Wednesday.* The twelve hundred men removed from Beaulieu and
went into camp three miles from Savannah.   They were divided into
three commands, as follows, that of the General in the centre, towards
Mishow, that of Dillon on the right, at *Jonshauss*, and that of Noailles
on the left, at *Brisqhauw*.
     Since the eleventh of September when the landing of our troops
was effected, variable north-west and north-east winds, prevailing
violently, prevented the continuance of the debarkation.   Most
of the long boats, two of which were lost, had not returned from
the shore.   To-day the sea is beautiful and all the boats are filled with
troops.

1779.   General Lincoln arrives with fifteen hundred American troops.[1] He camps near by and to the left of the division of Noailles.

Sept.
15th.

Saturday. M. D'Estaing, accompanied by the *Grenadiers* of Auxerrois and the *Chasseurs* of Champagne and of Guadeloupe, summons General Prevost to surrender.[2] He asks twelve hours time[3] to consider the proposition, and takes advantage of this interval to introduce into the

---

[1] The 12th and 13th were occupied in crossing the American troops, commanded by General Lincoln, over the Savannah river at Zubly's ferry. On the afternoon of the 13th, the troops from Augusta, under General McIntosh, formed a junction with them. Being advised on the 15th that Count D'Estaing had landed and that he would that night take post nine miles from Savannah, General Lincoln moved with his entire command and encamped at Cherokee Hill. The following day the French and American forces were united for future joint operations against the city. The enemy having destroyed the boats on the Savannah river, considerable delay was encountered by General Lincoln in effecting a crossing with his command at Zubly's ferry. But one canoe being found at first, and General Lincoln being extremely anxious to throw some cavalry across the river so that they could reconnoitre and follow the movements of the enemy, Pulaski accomplished this object by sending one man at a time, with his accoutrements, in this canoe and swimming the horse alongside. " In this manner" says Captain Bentalou, " between twenty and thirty horse accomplished a landing on the other bank, of whom Pulaski gave me the command." With this little force Captain Bentalou at once pressed forward, finding the advanced posts of the enemy evacuated, until late in the evening of the next day he came in sight of the British lines around Savannah. About twelve o'clock the same night he was joined by Count Pulaski with the rest of the Legion and some volunteers. Early in the morning an express was overtaken with a letter from Count D'Estaing to General Lincoln, and also one to Pulaski in which, after informing him of his landing, he said, among other flattering things, " that knowing Count Pulaski was there, he was sure he would be the first to join him." Although it rained heavily, Pulaski instantly hastened to Beaulieu where he found D'Estaing, and where, in the language of Captain Bentalou, the two " cordially embraced and expressed mutual happiness at the meeting." The junction of General Lincoln's forces with those of Count D'Estaing, before Savannah, was effected on the 16th. See Letter of General Lincoln to Congress, under date, Charleston, October 22, 1779.

[2] This demand was made by Count D'Estaing before General Lincoln had effected a junction with him. " Count D'Estaing summons his Excellency, General Prevost, to surrender himself to the Arms of his Majesty the King of France." The Count was flushed with the victory which he had recently won by the defeat of Lord Macartney at Grenada. Compare *Journal of the Siege of Savannah, Rivington's Royal Gazette,* No. 334, Dec. 11, 1779.

[3] A truce of only twelve hours seems to have been originally contemplated. It was subsequently extended, however, until the afternoon of the 17th.

1779. city Colonel Maitland, with six hundred Scotchmen whom he had brought from Port Royal.[1]   Finally Prevost answers that he has decided to defend himself.[2]

Sept.   *Monday.* The squadron of M. de Broves resumes its anchorage.   The
20th.   frigates *La Fortunée* and *La Blanche* anchor off Ossaba in the division of M. de la Motte-piquet.   They observe on board the General's ship the signal to land their troops: which command is executed.

21st.   *Tuesday.* During this, and the succeeding seven or eight days, fresh troops from the fleet arrive in camp.

22nd.   *Wednesday.* At seven o'clock in the morning our camp is moved to

---

[1] Colonel Maitland was at Beaufort when he was summoned to the relief of Savannah. He brought with him a detachment of about eight hundred men.   Lieutenant Colonel Cruger, with his small command, had previously repaired from Sunbury and united his forces with those of General Prevost.

[2] " On the evening of the 16th Colonel Maitland arrived at Dawfuskie, and, finding the passage up the river in possession of the French, he was obliged to resort to some other way of getting into the town.   While he was embarrassed in this difficulty, fortune threw into his hands some negro fishermen who were well acquainted with all the creeks through the marsh, and who informed him of a passage called Wall's cut, through Scull creek, by which small boats could pass at high water.   The tide and a thick fog favored the execution of his plans and enabled him with great difficulty to get through.   On the ensuing afternoon he reached the town, unperceived by the French.   The acquisition of this formidable reënforcement, headed by an experienced and brave officer, effected a complete change in the dispirited garrison.   A signal was made, and three cheers given which rung from one end of the town to the other." [*M'Call's History of Georgia*, vol. II, p. 255.] Compare *Rivington's Royal Gazette*, No. 334, Dec. 11, 1779.

Thus strengthened, Prevost who had procrastinated in order that he might concentrate within the lines of Savannah this formidable detachment with its gallant and experienced commander, immediately responded " the unanimous Determination has been that though we cannot look upon our Post as absolutely impregnable yet, that it may and ought to be defended : therefore, the evening Gun to be fired this Evening, at an Hour before Sundown, shall be the Signal for recommencing Hostilities, agreeable to your Excellency's Proposal."   During the Confederate struggle for Independence, this Wall's cut afforded the United States Gun Boats the means of entering Savannah river in the rear of Fort Pulaski. without encountering the fire of its batteries ; thereby completely isolating that fortification, and covering Federal working parties engaged in the erection of investing batteries at Venus's point and on the north end of Bird's island.

1779. a locality six hundred toises [1200 yards] distant from the city of Savannah. This city, situated on the southern bank of a river of the same name, appears to be built, with considerable regularity, of wood and brick, upon a uniform plain with a sandy soil, and is bounded on the south by a forest of thinly scattered pines, and on the north by the river Savannah. From east to west it has an extent of about six hundred toises [1200 yards], and in depth is considerably narrower. It did not seem to us that it possessed public buildings other than a temple [church] which occupies a central position.[1] On the right and left are two swamps which render it inaccessible from those directions. The enemy, with a frigate carrying nine-pounder guns, and two galleys armed with eighteen pounder guns, stationed in the river at the western extremity of the city, had nothing to fear from the rear, or from the right and left. It was necessary therefore to provide for the defense only of the front or southern exposure of the city. Here the enemy had an entrenchment and several batteries, the approach to this entrenchment being defended by *abatis*, *palissades*, and *chevaux de frise*. These works were strengthened by three redoubts placed triangularly at the extremity or western part of the line, and two mortar batteries, each mounting three or four pieces, which afforded a cross fire with two other redoubts erected in advance of the left of the entrenchments. Such was the situation of the enemy at the time of our arrival; but the English improved the interval employed by us in the erection of our counter batteries, by strengthening their position and by throwing up new works.

Our army which had taken up the line of march at seven o'clock in the morning to form a new camp six hundred toises [1200 yards] distant from the city, arrived at eight o'clock at the place of encampment. It was a wood of scattered pines through which we could observe the

---

[1] The reference is probably to *Christ Church* ; that is the *original building*, which occupied the site of the present structure. The city of Savannah could not, at this time, boast of more than four hundred and thirty houses. Using the present names of the streets, its boundaries were the *Bay* on the north, *Lincoln street* on the east, *South Broad street* on the south, and *Jefferson street* on the west. Outside the limits indicated, were some scattering houses ; particularly to the east and west.

1779. houses of Savannah.   Here the trees were cut down for a space sufficient to accommodate the encampment, which occupied about sixteen
hundred toises (3200 yards), commencing at the swamp to the enemy's
right, or on the west of tlie city, and extending to the swamp on his left,
or on the east of the city.   Quiet reigned on the northern side of the
city looking toward the river, in which the armed store-ship *La Truite*,
carrying a battery of twelve pounder guns, and the two galleys mounting eighteen and twenty-four pounder guns, had a second time taken
position to hold in check the English frigate and two galleys which constituted the only force the enemy had in that quarter.

The sole intention of the General was so to dispose his army as to
completely invest the city on its southern side.   The American troops,
numbering twelve hundred militia, two regiments, and one hundred
and thirty hussars and dragoons commanded by Count Pulaski, were
encamped on the right of the city, resting upon the swamp which borders it on that side.   The division of M. de Noailles, composed of nine
hundred men of the regiments of Champagne, Auxerrois, Foix, Guadeloupe and Martinique, camped to the right of the Americans.

The General's division, comprising one thousand men of the regiments
of Cambresis, Hainault, the volunteers of Berges, Agenois, Gatinois,
the Cape, and Port au Prince, and the artillery, was on the right of the
division of Noailles and formed the centre of the French army.

Dillon's division, composed of nine hundred men of the regiments of
Dillon, Armagnac, and the Volunteer Grenadiers, was posted on the
right of the General.

To the right of Dillon's division were the powder magazine, the cat-
tle depot, and a small field hospital.

On the right and a little in advance of the depot were the quarters
of the dragoons of Condé and of Belzunce, numbering fifty men and
commanded by M. Dejean.

Upon the same alignment and to the right of the dragoons, was **M.**
de Rouvrai with his Volunteer Chasseurs numbering seven hundred and
fifty men.

1779. To the right, and one hundred toises [200 yards] in advance of M. de Rouvrai, was M. Des Framais, commanding the Grenadier Volunteers and two hundred men of different regiments. He effectually closed the right of our army and rested upon the swamp which bounded the city on the east, or its left.

One perceives from these dispositions that Savannah was completely shut in from the front, in rear, and on each side.

Independently of the frigate *La Truite*[1] and the two galleys which had reascended the river until within cannon shot of the city, the frigate *La Chimère* and the armed store ship *La Bricole,* which it was found impossible to carry up the river to a point whence the city could be bombarded, served to cut off all communications with the islands formed by the numerous river-mouths which bathe the coast of Georgia.

Having established our camp, we took possession of a large and beautiful house, distant two leagues from the city and situated at a place called Thunder-bolt bluff[2] on the bank of an outlet of the Savannah river, that we might here locate our hospital. This served afterwards as the point from which we communicated with the fleet; it being more accessible and nearer than Beaulieu, which was abandoned.

Sept. 22nd. *Wednesday,* at nine o'clock in the evening, M. de Noailles orders M. de Guillaume, lieutenant of Grenadiers in the regiment of Guadeloupe, with fifty men detailed from the different regiments composing the division of Noailles, to take possession of an advanced post of the enemy. M. Guillaume, carried away by his courage, disregards the instructions of the Viscount de Noailles and, being incautious, rushes straight upon the enemy, attacking with full force a post which should have been captured by surprise. The enemy perceives and baffles his attempt. He is repulsed by a very lively fire of artillery and musketry. M. de Noailles, who followed closely to support him, appears in person on the spot and

---

[1] This vessel anchored in the Back river, nearly opposite the city of Savannah, and fired across the eastern end of Hutchinson's island. The galleys were posted lower down the river and within cannon shot of the enemy's eastern lines.

[2] In the MS. written *Tunderbullblof.*

1779. seeing that success was impossible, orders a retreat during which we lose four soldiers of the regiment of Guadeloupe. M. de Grangies, a second lieutenant of the regiment of Port au Prince, who was with him, and several men are wounded.

On this occasion M. Roger, of the advanced guard, has two men killed and two wounded.

Sept. 23rd.   *Thursday.* At three o'clock P.M. a trench is opened one hundred and fifty toises [300 yards] from the enemy's works. Six companies of picked troops are detailed for the protection of the working parties, who complete their labors before daylight without being disturbed by the enemy who had not observed their operations.

M. de Rouvrai, colonel of the Volunteer Chasseurs, commanded in the stead of M. de Dillon who was sick to-day. He had for his second officer M. Odune, lieutenant colonel of the army.

24th.   *Friday.* At seven o'clock in the morning, when a thick fog which arose at daylight had disappeared, the enemy perceived our works and made a sortie with six hundred men to attack us. They are repulsed at the point of the bayonet and driven back to their entrenchments. Our imprudence in leaving our trench to pursue them exposed us to the artillery fire of their redoubts and batteries, and caused the loss of seventy men killed and wounded; among whom were several officers. It is believed that the enemy sustained a loss equally great.[1]

M. de Saucé, an artillery officer, reconnoiters a position on the left

[1] The English accounts affirm that this sortie was made with three companies of Light Infantry, under Major Graham, for the purpose of enticing the French out of their lines so that something like a correct estimate of the besieging forces might be formed. It is claimed that the scheme succeeded. Major Graham was pursued by a heavy column of French soldiers who, pressing him closely, were drawn within range of the English batteries which delivered a galling fire. The British acknowledge a loss of twenty-one killed and wounded. Among the former was Lieutenant McPherson of the 71st regiment.

See also, *Ramsay's History of the Revolution, etc.*, vol. II, p. 37. Trenton, MDCCLXXXV.

Compare *Rivington's Royal Gazette*, No. 334, Dec. 11, 1779, in which the English casualties are reported at "1 Subaltern and 3 Privates killed, and 15 wounded." The French loss is estimated at "14 Officers and 145 Privates killed and wounded."

1779. of our trench suitable for the location of a battery. He commences its construction at night fall, and completes it before day.

Sept. 25th. At seven o'clock on Saturday morning this battery, with four embrasures in which only two eighteen pounder guns had been mounted, opens fire upon the city with little effect. Nevertheless, the General orders this battery to be remodelled so as to mount twelve 18 and 12 pounder guns : further, that another battery, to contain thirteen 18 pounder guns, should be constructed on the right of the trench, and that no firing should take place until everything was finished. He also directed that a bomb battery of nine mortars should be located one hundred toises [200 yards] to the left and a little in rear of the trench, by the side of which it was decided to erect a battery of six 16 pounder guns for the Americans.

27th. *Monday.* At one o'clock in the morning, the enemy sends a strong detachment to make a close reconnoissance of our trench. It is discovered and compelled to retire.

The same day we are informed in camp of the capture of the ship Experiment,[1] of fifty-four guns, by the *Sagittaire*. She was loaded with supplies for Savannah, with wine, beer, rum, cloth, and seven hundred thousand pounds of army rations. She also carried a general officer[2] who was to have supplanted Prevost in the command of Savannah.

We commence the battery on the right of the trench, at the same time vigorously pushing the construction of that on the left, and prosecuting our work upon the bomb battery. The enemy does not perceive our operations, and gives us but little annoyance. At half past twelve o'clock at night a patrol, composed of some of our soldiers and workmen, causes a very sad mistake. Despite the precautions of M. de Pont-devaux, the officer of the day, and M. de Trécesson, second in

---

[1] This ship, commanded by Sir James Wallace, was captured on the 24th. Having lost her bow-sprit and masts in a gale encountered during her passage from New York, she could offer but feeble resistance.

[2] Major General Garth.

1779. command, we were unable to prevent the troops in the trenches, who were under the impression that they saw the enemy approaching in force, from delivering a heavy fire upon our working parties, which entailed upon us a loss of fifteen men, killed and wounded. The same error is repeated at four o'clock in the morning, the fire from the trenches being however, of shorter duration and less lively, and the laborers on this occasion suffering a loss of only two men. The alarm created by this firing spreads through our camp, and M. de Noailles advances, with his division in column, through the mortar battery to a point between the trenches and the city with the intention of intercepting the sortie. He ascertains the mistake and causes his troops to return.[1]

Oct. 2nd.   *Saturday.* The ship *La Truite* and the galleys open a heavy cannonade upon the city with little effect.

3rd. to 4th.   At midnight, on *Monday,* the bombardment begins.[2] It ceases at

[1] Captain M'Call* gives us a different version of this affair. He says : " On the night of the 27th Major Archibald M'Arthur, with a detachment of the 71st regiment, made a sortie to attack the allies in some batteries which they were constructing to mount some heavy cannon. After commencing the attack briskly, he retired unperceived. The French attempted to gain his left flank, and the Americans his right. M'Arthur retired so suddenly and silently that the right and left of the allies commenced a brisk fire upon each other, and several lives were lost before the mistake was discovered.

[2] The allied army opened the bombardment with fifty three pieces of heavy cannon and fourteen mortars. *Stedman's History of the American War,* vol. II, p. 127. London, 1794. Compare *Lee's Memoirs, etc.,* vol. I, p. 103, Philadelphia, 1812. Dr. Ramsay states that " the besiegers opened with nine mortars, thirty-seven pieces of cannon from the landside, and sixteen from the water." *History of the Revolution, etc.,* vol. II, p. 38. Trenton, MDCCLXXXV. Compare *Gordon's History of the United States, etc.,* vol. III, p. 328. London, MDCCLXXXVIII. *Marshall's Life of Washington,* vol. IV, p. 99. Philadelphia, 1805.

By a shell from the bomb battery of 9 mortars, Ensign Pollard of the Second Battalion of Gen. De Lancey's Brigade was killed in a house on the Bay. A daughter of Mrs. Thompson was killed in the same locality by a solid shot.

In commenting upon the effect of the bombardment, T. W. Moore, who was an aid-de-

* *History of Georgia,* vol. II, p. 259. See also *Stedman's History of the American War,* vol. II, p. 127, London, 1794. *Ramsay's History of the Revolution etc.,* vol. II, p. 38, Trenton, MDCCLXXXV. *Gordon's History of the United States, etc.,* vol. III, p. 328, London, MDCCLXXXVIII.

1779. two o'clock, by order of M. de Noailles, because the mis-directed bombs fell in great numbers in the trench which he commanded. This bad firing was occasioned by a mistake of a ship's steward who had sent to the cannoneers a keg of rum instead of a keg of beer.

Oct. 4th. *Monday.* At four o'clock in the morning, the enemy's beat of drum at day-break furnishes the signal for unmasking our batteries on the right and left of the trench, and that of the Americans to the left of the mortar battery, and we begin to cannonade and bombard the city and the enemy's works with more vivacity than precision. The cannoneers being still under the influence of rum, their excitement did not allow them to direct their pieces with proper care. Besides, our projectiles did little damage to works which were low and constructed of sand. The effect of this very violent fire was fatal only to the houses and to some women who occupied them.[1]

Protected by their entrenchments, the enemy could not have lost many men, if we may judge from the effect of their fire upon our works which had been constructed hastily, and with far less skill and care than theirs.[2]

All our batteries ceased firing at eight o'clock in the morning that we might repair our left battery which had been shaken to pieces by its own fire. A dense fog favors our workmen. We open fire again

camp to General Prevost during the siege, says that the town was torn to pieces by the shells and shot, and that the shrieks of women and children were heard on every side. " Many poor creatures," he adds, " were killed in trying to get in their cellars, or hide themselves under the bluff of Savannah river."

[1] During the progress of the siege, considerable damage was done to buildings and personal property in the town of Savannah, by the fire from the investing batteries. Among other premises, the quarters of Anthony Stokes, Chief Justice of the colony, were burned by a shell from the allied army, and most of his papers were destroyed. *View of the Constitution of the British Colonies, etc.,* Preface iii, also p. 116. London, MDCCLXXXIII.

[2] In order to avoid the projectiles, Governor Sir James Wright and Lieutenant Governor John Graham, on the 4th of October, moved out of the town and occupied a tent next to Colonel Maitland's, on the right of the British lines.

1779. at ten o'clock in the morning, and continue it with little intermission until four o'clock after midnight.[1]

Oct. 6th. Cannonading and bombarding at long intervals. We begin to lose confidence upon discovering that all this heavy firing will not render the assault less difficult. We should not have constructed works. In doing so we afforded the English time to strengthen theirs. We regret that we did not attack on the very first day.[2]

7th. *Thursday.* A very lively cannonade. We bombard and throw carcasses into Savannah which set the city on fire for the third time.

[1] The bombardment of the 5th was unusually severe. " A Mulatto Man and three Negroes were killed in the Lieutenant Governor's Cellar. In the Evening, the House of the Late Mrs. Lloyd, near the Church, was burnt by a shell, and seven Negroes lost their Lives in it. Whilst the House was on Fire, one of the hottest Cannonadings they had yet made was kept up to prevent People from extinguishing the Flames. In the Night another Shell fell through Mr. Laurie's House in Broughton Street, which killed two Women and two Children who were under it." *Rivington's Royal Gazette*, No. 334, Dec. 11, 1779.

[2] When the French fleet first appeared off the Georgia coast the English had but twenty-three pieces of cannon mounted upon their works around Savannah. On the day of the assault one hundred and twenty-three guns were in position.* Intelligent British officers, who were present during the siege, admitted that the French army alone could have carried the city in ten minutes, without the aid of artillery, had the assault been made at the earliest moment.

The energy and skill displayed by the English in strengthening their old works, in erecting new ones, in dismantling the vessels of war in the river and placing their guns in battery to the south, east, and west of Savannah, and, above all, the introduction of Colonel Maitland's forces into the city at a most opportune moment, reflect great credit upon those charged with the defense.

If, instead of parleying, D'Estaing had insisted upon an immediate response to his summons for surrender, the probabilities are that Prevost would have acceded to his demand. Had he refused, there is little doubt but that the investing army could immediately have swept over the half finished entrenchments, and restored the capital of Georgia to the possession of the Revolutionists. Delay proved fatal to the enterprise.

* Stedman[a] asserts that when the French first landed " not more than ten or twelve pieces of artillery appeared upon the fortifications at Savannah ; but so incessantly did the garrison labor in strengthening and enlarging the old works, and in erecting new redoubts and batteries, that before the conclusion of the siege near one hundred pieces of cannon were mounted."

" On the approach of the French," says General Henry Lee, " few guns were mounted in the works of the Enemy ; but such had been the vast exertions of General Prevost, that now nearly one hundred of different calibers were in full array." *Memoirs, etc.*, vol. I, p. 103. Philadelphia, 1812.

[a] *History of the American War*, vol. II, p. 128. London, 1794.

1779.
Oct. 7.
We construct a new trench in advance of our left battery to persuade the enemy that we do not as yet contemplate an assault, but that our intention is to push our approaches up to his works.

8th.   *Friday.* We cannonade and bombard feebly. The enemy does little more. He seems to be husbanding his strength for the anticipated attack. Informed of all that transpires in our army, he is cognizant of the trifling effect produced by his fire upon us in our trenches. Everything forces us to the conclusion that we must, on the morrow, make a general assault upon the city. The length of time requisite for the operations of a siege, the exhaustion of the supplies of the fleet, and the pressing dangers resulting from our insecure anchorage decide the General to take this step.[1]

idem.   Prevost asks permission of M. D'Estaing to send from the city the women and children, several of whom had already been killed by our bombs and cannon balls.[2] To this request the Count returns a refusal.[3]

[1] On the morning of the 8th Major L'Enfant, with five men, despite a brisk fire from the British lines, succeeded in kindling the *abatis*. The dampness of the atmosphere however, and the moisture of the newly felled trees prevented the success of this bold undertaking. See *Ramsay's History of the Revolution, etc.*, vol. II, p. 38. Trenton MDCCLXXXV. Compare *Gordon's History of the United States, etc.*, vol. III, p. 328. London, MDCCLXXXVIII.

[2] Captain John Simpson of the Georgia Loyalists was killed by a grape shot, while walking in Major Wright's redoubt. During the day many houses were damaged. "The firing continued very hot all Night, and a great number of Shells were thrown, one of which fell into the Provost, killed two Men on the Spot, and wounded nine others, some of whom died since. Another burst in the Cellar, under the Office of the Commissioner of Claims, killed one Negro, and wounded another." *Rivington's Royal Gazette*, No. 334, Dec. 11, 1779.

[3] On the 29th of September "General McIntosh solicited General Lincoln's permission to send a flag, with a letter to General Provost, to obtain leave for Mrs. McIntosh and his family, and such other females and children as might choose, to leave the town during the siege or until the contest should be decided. Major John Jones, aid to General McIntosh, was the bearer of the flag and letter, and found Mrs. McIntosh and family in a cellar, where they had been confined several days. Indeed, those damp apartments furnished the only safe retreat for females and children during the siege General Provost refused to grant the request, imagining that it would restrain the besiegers from

1779.   *Saturday.* At midnight,[1] we take arms and the army is formed in
⌣
Oct.   three columns; the first, commanded by M. Dillon, under the General,
9th.   the second by M. de Steding, colonel of infantry, and the third, intended as a reserve corps, by the Viscount de Noailles. The Americans,
by themselves, constituted a third column of attack; and the troops in
the trenches, commanded by M. de Sablière, supported by the chasseurs
of Martinique, were to make a sortie for a feigned attack. The vanguard, under the command of M. de Betisy, moved in front of the
General's column. It was ordered to take possession of a redoubt on
the right capable of inflicting injury on the General's column which
would be obliged to pass it in making its attack upon the enemy's
entrenchments.

At this point the column of M. de Steding was to incline to the left,
separate itself from the other columns, cross the road leading to
Augusta, and assault a battery and the entrenchments on the enemy's
extreme right occupied by Scotch troops under the command of M. de
Maitland. The American column was to move above the Augusta
road and make its attack between the two French columns.

When these three columns, each divided into three battalions, should
respectively arrive at their different points of attack, they were directed
to form themselves so that they might present to the enemy three dis-
tinct heads of columns of attack. M. de Noailles, with his reserve

throwing bombs and carcasses among the houses to set them on fire." *M'Call's Georgia,*
vol. ii, p. 260.

Doubtless this refusal, coupled with the fact that Prevost had taken advantage of the
truce, consequent upon the demand for a surrender of the city, to strengthen his position
and introduce reinforcements, influenced the commanders of the allied army in rejecting
an application, so humane in its character, which otherwise would certainly have received
their immediate sanction. Such is the intimation given in the letter of refusal returned
by Count D'Estaing and General Lincoln.

"This humane request," says Dr. Ramsay,* was, from motives of policy, refused. The
combined army was so confident of success, that it was suspected a desire of secreting the
plunder lately taken from the inhabitants of South Carolina was a considerable object
covered under the specious veil of humanity. It was also presumed that a refusal would
expedite a surrender."

[1] i.e. at 12 o'clock P.M. on Friday.

History of the Revolution, etc., vol. ii, p. 38. Trenton, MDCCLXXXV.

1779. corps, was to occupy an eminence from which he could observe everything that should transpire. In the event of success he was to advance to the most suitable points; and, in case of a reverse, cover the retreat. He had field artillery with him.

By three o'clock in the morning all our dispositions had been perfected. At the head of M. de Steding's column were posted sixty volunteers selected from all the corps: and M. Roman, a Frenchman, and an officer of the American Artillery, was put in command of them. This officer assured us that he had built the defences of Savannah and was acquainted with all its environs.[1] He is charged with the conduct of this column. We commence marching by the left to attack the city on its right, where its western side, as we have before intimated, is fortified by three redoubts located triangularly. The troops in the trenches were ordered to make the false attack a quarter of an hour before day, and to engage the enemy prior to the commencement of the true attack. The columns marched by divisions, with easy gait and leisurely, that they might arrive at the point of attack at the designated hour.

Upon emerging from the woods M. de Steding asks M. Roman how far his point of attack was from the redoubt which the vanguard was

[1] M. Roman evidently referred to the fortifications which had been constructed by the Americans for the protection of Savannah, then the capital of Georgia, prior to the capture of the city by Colonel Campbell in December 1778. The resistance offered by General Howe, on this occasion, was feeble and confused. Unable to retain possession of the city, the Americans retired with a loss of about one hundred killed on the field or drowned in the retreat, and thirty-eight officers and four hundred and fifteen privates captured. Forty-eight cannon and twenty-three mortars fell into the hands of the enemy.* It would seem that for some time after this capture the English did not materially alter or strengthen the works which they found existing upon the eastern, western, and southern exposures of the city. Upon the appearance of the French fleet, however, the utmost activity was displayed. In addition to the garrison, between four and five hundred negroes were put to work upon the lines; and, so rapidly did the labor progress, that before the French and American batteries opened fire, the British had raised around the town thirteen substantial redoubts, and fifteen gun batteries, mounting eighty pieces of cannon. These batteries were manned by sailors from the Fowey, the Rose, and the Keppel, and by mariners and volunteers from other ships and transports in the river. Besides these guns in fixed positions, field pieces were distributed along the line.

*See *Ramsay's History of the Revolution, etc.*, vol. II, p. 6. Trenton, MDCCLXXXV.

1779. to assault.   M. Roman, who commanded these sixty volunteers simply in the capacity of a guide, replied he knew nothing beyond his own command, that he was unacquainted with the surroundings of the city, that the works had been altered since the enemy had taken possession of them, and that he would act as guide no longer.

At five o'clock in the morning the three columns, which had observed a similar order of march, arrived within about eighty toises [160 yards] of the edge of the wood which borders upon Savannah.   Here the head of column was halted and we were ordered to form into platoons. Day begins to dawn and we grow impatient.   This movement is scarcely commenced when we are directed to march forward, quick time, the vanguard inclining a little to the right, the column of M. de Steding to the left, and the column of the General moving straight to the front.   M. de Noailles, with his reserve corps, proceeds to a small eminence from which he could observe all our movements and repair to any point where the exigencies might demand his presence.

At half past five o'clock we hear on our right and on the enemy's left a very lively fire of musketry and of cannon upon our troops from the trenches who had commenced the false attack.[1]   A few minutes

[1] On the night of the 8th of October, James Curry, sergeant major of the Charleston Grenadiers, deserted to the enemy and communicated to the English the general plan of attack concerted by the commanders of the allied army.   Thus advised of the true character of the assault, and informed of the point where the genuine demonstration would be made, Prevost, leaving only a small force to guard the left of his works, concentrated his troops near the Spring-Hill and Ebenezer batteries, and placed Lieutenant Colonel Maitland in command of that portion of the line.   General Isaac Huger was ordered, with five hundred men drafted from "the militia of the first and second brigades, general Williamson's, and the first and second battalions of Charleston Militia," to march to the left of the enemy's lines and remain as near them as he possibly could, without being discovered, until four o'clock in the morning, at which time the troops from the trenches were to begin their attack upon the British entrenchments.   He was then to advance and attack as near the river as practicable.   Although this was intended simply as a feint, should a favorable opportunity offer, he was to improve it and push into the town.

After wading half a mile through the rice field which bordered the city on the east, General Huger reached his point of attack and, at the appointed time and place, made the assault.   The enemy was on the alert.   He was received with music and a heavy fire of cannon and musketry, before which he retreated with a loss of twenty-eight men.   No other demonstration was made by this command.   The attack by the troops from the

1779. afterwards we are discovered by the enemy's sentinels who fire a few shots. The General now orders an advance at double quick, to shout *Vive le Roy*, and to beat the charge.[1] The enemy opens upon us a very brisk fire of artillery and musketry which, however, does not prevent the vanguard from advancing upon the redoubt, and the right column upon the entrenchments. The ardor of our troops and the difficulties offered by the ground do not permit us long to preserve our ranks. Disorder begins to prevail. The head of the column penetrates within the entrenchments but, having marched too quickly, is not supported by the rest of the column which, arriving in confusion, is cut down by discharges of grape shot from the redoubts and batteries, and the musketry fire from the entrenchments. We are violently repulsed at this point; and, instead of moving to the right, this [Dillon's] column and the vanguard fall back toward the left. Count D'Estaing receives a musket shot almost within the redoubt, and M. Betizi is here several times wounded.

The column of M. de Steding, which moved to the left, while traversing a muddy swamp full of brambles, loses its formation and no longer preserves any order. This swamp, upon which the enemy's entrenchments rested, formed a slope which served as a glacis to them. The firing is very lively; and, although this column is here most seriously injured, it crosses the road to Augusta that it may advance to the enemy's right which it was ordered to attack. On this spot nearly all the Volunteers are killed. The Baron de Steding is here wounded.

---

trenches, upon the centre of the British lines, was feebly maintained and produced no impression. It was repulsed by the troops under the command of Lieutenant Colonel Hamilton of the North Carolina regiment of Loyalists.

[1] Dr. Ramsay* asserts that the real attack upon the Spring-Hill battery was made with three thousand five hundred French troops, six hundred Continentals, and three hundred and fifty of the Charleston Militia.

To the brave and accomplished soldier, Lieutenant Colonel Maitland, did General Prevost assign the defense of his right, the post of honor and of danger.

History of the Revolution, etc., vol. II, p. 39. Trenton, MDCCLXXXV. Compare *Marshall's Life of Washington*, vol. IV, p. 101. Philadelphia, 1805.

This statement of the strength of the assaulting columns is adopted by Dr. Gordon. (*History of the United States, etc.*, vol. III, p. 330. London, MDCCLXXXVIII.)

1779. The column of M. D'Estaing, and the repulsed vanguard which had retreated to the left, arrived here as soon as the column of M. de Steding
and threw it into utter confusion. At this moment everything is in
such disorder that the formations are no longer preserved. The road
to Augusta is choked up. It here, between two impracticable morasses,
consists of an artificial causeway upon which all our soldiers, who had
disengaged themselves from the swamps, collected. We are crowded
together and badly pressed. Two eighteen pounder guns, upon field
carriages, charged with cannister and placed at the head of the road,
cause terrible slaughter. The musketry fire from the entrenchments
is concentrated upon this spot and upon the swamps. Two English
galleys and one frigate[1] sweep this point with their broadsides, and the
redoubts and batteries use only grape shot which they shower down
upon this locality. Notwithstanding all this, our officers endeavor to
form into columns this mass which does not retreat, and the soldiers
themselves strive to regain their ranks. Scarcely have they commenced
to do this, when the General orders the charge to be beaten. Three
times do our troops advance *en masse* up to the entrenchments which
cannot be carried.[2] An attempt is made to penetrate through the
swamp on our left to gain the enemy's right. More than half of those
who enter are either killed or remain stuck fast in the mud.

The American column advanced, in good order, to its point of attack.
At the first discharge of a gun, two-thirds of the Virginia militia detach
themselves from it. Only three hundred men of the regular regiments
and Pulaski's dragoons remain ; and, although repulsed with severe loss,

[1] The armed brig Germaine delivered a galling fire.
[2] The few casualties reported in the British ranks, and the terrible slaughter with
which the assaulting columns were punished, advise us how admirably Prevost had protected his troops by entrenchments and redoubts, and how skillfully and rapidly the
besieged handled their muskets and field and siege pieces.

The loss sustained by the English was remarkably small. General Prevost reported
40 killed, 63 wounded, 4 missing, 48 deserted : total 155. Captain T. W. Moore, aid
to General Prevost, in a letter to his wife under date Savannah, November 4th, 1779,
estimates the entire loss in killed, wounded, and missing during the siege, at 163 ; and
Stedman says, " the loss of the garrison, in the whole, did not exceed one hundred and
twenty."

1779. return repeatedly to the assault, thus furnishing a brilliant illustration of their valor.[1]

[1] The participation by the American forces in this memorable assault is so sadly ignored by our unknown writer, that, in the interest of truth and as a proper supplement to the narrative, we cannot refrain from presenting the following extract from an account prepared by Major Thomas Pinckney* who was present and an earnest actor in the bloody details of this unfortunate and ill-considered attempt.

" The French troops were to be divided into three columns, the Americans into two, the heads of which were to be posted in a line, with proper intervals at the edge of the wood adjoining the open space of five or six hundred yards between it and the enemy's line, and at four o'clock in the morning, a little before daylight, the whole was, on a signal being given, to rush forward and attack the redoubts and batteries opposed to their front.

" The American column of the right, which adjoined the French, were to be preceded by Pulaski, with his cavalry and the cavalry of South Carolina, and were to follow the French until they approach the edge of the wood, when they were to break off and take their position.

" This column was composed of the Light Infantry under Colonel Laurens, of the 2d Regiment of South Carolina, and the 1st Battalion of Charleston Militia. The second American column consisted of the 1st and 5th South Carolina Regiments, commanded by Brigadier General McIntosh of Georgia. A corps of French West India Troops, under the Viscompte de Noailles, the Artillery, and some American Militia, formed the reserve under General Lincoln.

" A faint attack by the South Carolina Militia and Georgians, under Brigadier General Huger, was ordered to be made on the enemy's left; but, instead of the French troops being paraded so as to march off at four o'clock, it was near four before the head of that column reached our front. The whole army then marched towards the skirt of the wood in one long column, and as they approached the open space were to break off into the different columns, as ordered, for the attack. But, by the time the first French column had arrived at the open space, the day had fairly broke, when Count D'Estaing, without waiting until the other columns had arrived at their position, placed himself at the head of the first column and rushed forward to the attack. But this body was so severely galled by the grape shot from the batteries as they advanced, and by both grape shot and musketry when they reached the Abbatis, that, in spite of the effort of the officers, the column got into confusion and broke away to their left toward the wood in that direction; the second and the third French columns shared successively the same fate, having the additional discouragement of seeing as they marched to the attack, the repulse and loss of their comrades who had preceded them.

" Count Pulaski who, with the cavalry, preceded the right column of the Americans, proceeded gallantly until stopped by the Abbatis, and, before he could force through it, received his mortal wound. In the meantime, Colonel Laurens, at the head of the Light Infantry, followed by the 2d South Carolina Regiment and 1st Battalion Charleston

*See *Garden's Anecdotes of the American Revolution.* Field's reprint, vol. III, p. 22. Brooklyn, 1865.

5

1779.   General Pulaski here receives a long barreled musket shot in his thigh.[1]

Militia, attacked the Spring-Hill redoubt, got into the ditch and planted the colors of the 2d Regiment on the berm, but the parapet was too high for them to scale it under so heavy a fire, and, after much slaughter, they were driven out of the ditch.   When General Pulaski was about to be removed from the field, Colonel D. Horry, to whom the command of the cavalry devolved, asked what were his directions.   He answered, 'follow my Lancers to whom I have given my order of attack.'   But the Lancers were so severely galled by the enemy's fire, that they also inclined off to the left and were followed by all the cavalry, breaking through the American column who were attacking the Spring Hill redoubt.   By this time the 2d American column, headed by General McIntosh, to which I was attached, arrived at the foot of the Spring-Hill redoubt, and such a scene of confusion as there appeared, is not often equalled.   Colonel Laurens had been separated from that part of his command that had not entered the Spring-Hill ditch by the cavalry who had borne it before them into the swamp to the left, and when we marched up, inquired *if we had seen them.*   Count D'Estaing was wounded in the arm, and endeavouring to rally his men, a few of whom with a drummer he had collected.   General McIntosh did not speak French, but desired me to inform the commander-in-chief that his column was fresh and that he wished his directions where, under present circumstances, he should make the attack.   The Count ordered that we should move more to the left, and by no means to interfere with the troops he was endeavoring to rally; in pursuing this direction we were thrown too much to the left, and before we could reach Spring-Hill redoubt, we had to pass through Yamacraw swamp, then wet and boggy, with the galley at the mouth annoying our left flank with grape shot.   While struggling through this morass, the firing slacked, and it was reported that the whole army had retired.   I was sent by General McIntosh to look out from the Spring-Hill, where I found not an assailant standing.   On reporting this to the General, he ordered a retreat which was effected without much loss, notwithstanding the heavy fire of grape shot with which we were followed."

Perhaps the most intelligent and soldierly account of the operations during the siege of Savannah, and of the causes which conspired to bring about the signal disaster encountered by the allied army, is that penned by General Henry Lee.*   His *résumé* is comprehensive, his military criticisms are just.

[1] Captain McCall says (*History of Georgia*, vol. II, p. 267):   "Count Pulaski attempted to pass the works into the town, and received *a small cannon shot* in the groin, of which he fell near the abattis."   Dr. Stevens (*History of Georgia*, vol. II, p. 235,) asserts that when Pulaski fell before the lines of Savannah, he was carried back a little distance, and that Dr. James Lynah of Charleston extracted from his groin an *iron grape shot.*   The operation, which was exceedingly painful, was borne by Pulaski "with inconceivable fortitude."   This grape shot, as late as 1859, was said to have been still in the possession of the Lynah family.

Colonel Paul Bentalou (*Pulaski vindicated etc.*, p. 29), affirms that Pulaski, while

[1] *Memoirs of the War in the Southern Department*, vol. I, pp. 99–112.   Philadelphia, 1812.   Compare *Botta's History of the War of the Independence of the United States of America*, vol. II, pp. 203–210. New Haven, 1836. *Marshall's Life of Washington*, vol. IV, p. 95, *et seq*: Philadelphia, 1805.

1779. Standing in the road leading to Augusta, and at a most exposed point, the General, with perfect self-possession, surveys this slaughter, demands constant renewals of the assault and, although sure of the bravery of his troops, determines upon a retreat only when he sees that success is impossible.

We beat a retreat which is mainly effected across the swamp lying to the right of the Augusta road ; our forces being entirely, and at short

attempting to penetrate to the French column under D'Estaing which, in the swamp, was subjected to a murderous fire, received a *swivel shot* in the upper part of his right thigh. After the assault was over, he '' was conveyed on board the United States brig, the *Wasp*, to go round to Charleston. They remained some days in the Savannah river ; and, during that time, the most skillful surgeons in the French fleet attended on Count Pulaski. It was found impossible to establish suppuration, and gangrene was the consequence. Just as the *Wasp* got out of the river Pulaski breathed his last, and the corpse immediately became so offensive that his officer [Captain Bentalou] was compelled, though reluctantly, to consign to a watery grave all that was now left upon earth of his beloved and honored commander.''

Major Rogowski thus describes Pulaski's final charge. '' For half an hour the guns roared and blood flowed abundantly. Seeing an opening between the enemy's works Pulaski resolved, with his Legion and a small detachment of Georgia cavalry, to charge through, enter the city, confuse the enemy, and cheer the inhabitants with good tidings. General Lincoln approved the daring plan. Imploring the help of the Almighty, Pulaski shouted to his men '' Forward,'' and we, two hundred strong, rode at full speed after him, the earth resounding under the hoofs of our chargers. For the first two minutes all went well. We sped like Knights into the peril. Just, however, as we passed the gap between the two batteries, a cross fire, like a pouring shower, confused our ranks. I looked around. Oh ! sad moment, ever to be remembered ! Pulaski lies prostrate on the ground. I leaped towards him, thinking possibly his wound was not dangerous, but a *canister shot* had pierced his thigh, and the blood was also flowing from his breast, probably from a second wound. Falling on my knees I tried to raise him. He said in a faint voice. Jesus ! Maria ! Joseph ! Further, I knew not, for at that moment a musket ball grazing my scalp blinded me with blood, and I fell to the ground in a state of insensibility.'' * * * * *

In *Rivington's Gazette*, Count Pulaski is said to have been mortally wounded by '' *a Grape shot in his Groin.*''

Count Pulaski, at the head of two hundred horsemen, was in full gallop riding into the town, between the redoubts, with an intention of charging in the rear, when he received a mortal wound. Such is the language of Dr. Ramsay,* writing only a few years after the death of this intrepid partisan.

* *History of the Revolution, etc.,* vol. II, p. 40. Trenton, MDCCLXXXV. Compare Dr. Gordon's *History of the United States, etc.,* vol. III, p. 330. London, MDCCLXXXVIII. *Marshall's Life of Washington,* vol. IV, p. 102. Philadelphia, 1805.

1779. range, exposed to the concentrated fire of the entrenchments which constantly increases in vehemence. At this juncture the enemy show themselves openly upon the parapets, and deliver their fire with their muskets almost touching our troops. The General here receives a second shot.[1]

About four hundred men, more judiciously led by the Baron de Steding, retreated without loss by following the road to Augusta and turning the swamp by a long détour.

M. de Noailles, anxious to preserve his command for the moment when it could be used to best advantage, orders his reserve corps to fall back rapidly. Unless he had done this it would have suffered a loss almost as severe as that encountered by the assaulting columns, the effect of the grape shot being more dangerous at the remove where it was posted than at the foot of the entrenchments. Accompanied only by his adjutant, he ascends an elevation fifteen paces in advance of his corps that he might with certainty observe all the movements of the army. His Adjutant, M. Calignon, is mortally wounded by his side.

When the Viscount de Noailles perceives the disorder reigning in the columns, he brings his reserve corps up to charge the enemy : and, when he hears the retreat sounded, advances in silence, at a slow step and in perfect order, to afford an opportunity to the repulsed troops to reform themselves in his rear. He makes a demonstration to penetrate

---

[1] After the retreat of the assaulting columns from the right of the British lines, eighty men lay dead in the ditch and on the parapet of the redoubt first attacked, and ninety-three within the abattis. The attack upon the Ebenezer Battery, the Spring-Hill redoubt, and on the redoubt in which Colonel Maitland had located his head-quarters, was made with the utmost gallantry and impetuosity. Two standards were planted by the allied forces upon the Ebenezer redoubt ; one of which was captured, and the other brought off by the brave Sergeant Jasper, at the moment suffering from a mortal wound.

Count D'Estaing, during the conduct of this assault, received two musket shots, one in the arm and the other in the thigh.

"The Ditch," says an eye witness, " was filled with Dead, and in Front, for 50 yards, the Field was covered with Slain. Many hung dead and wounded on the Abattis ; and for some hundred yards without the Lines, the Plain was strewed with mangled Bodies, killed by our Grape and Langridge."

1779. within the entrenchments in case the enemy should leave them, and prepares to cut them off in that event. Under these circumstances he encounters some loss, but the anticipated sortie would have caused the total destruction of our army. That the enemy did not make this apprehended sortie is to be attributed to this excellent disposition of his forces, and this prompt manœuvre on the part of the Viscount de Noailles.[1]

The fragments of the army hastily form in single column behind the reserve corps, and begin marching to our camp. M. de Noailles constitutes the rear guard and retires slowly and in perfect order.

Towards eight o'clock in the morning the army was again in camp, and a cessation of hostilities for the purpose of burying the dead and removing the wounded was proposed and allowed.[2]

Upon an inspection of the returns, the Major General ascertained that we had lost in killed and wounded.

French soldiers,	760	men	
French officers,	61	"	total, 1133.[3]
Americans	312	"	

[1] Major Glasier of the 60th regiment who, with the grenadiers and reserve marines, was supporting the points assailed, did make a sortie from the British lines when the order for retreat was given by the commander of the allied army. He struck General McIntosh's column in the flank and pursued the retiring troops as far as the abattis.

See *M'Call's History of Georgia*, vol. II, p. 268. Compare *Lee's Memoirs of the War in the Southern Department, etc.*, vol. I, p. 108. Philadelphia, 1812. *Marshall's Life of Washington*, vol IV, p. 102. Philadelphia, 1805.

[2] This truce lasted from ten o'clock in the morning, until four P.M.

[3] The aggregate loss encountered by the allied army during the progress of the siege and in the assault of the 9th of October, has been variously estimated from one thousand to fifteen hundred, killed and wounded. Dr. Ramsay (*History of the Revolution, etc.*, vol. II, p. 40, Trenton, MDCCLXXXV) asserts, that the assaulting columns under Count D'Estaing and General McIntosh did not stand the enemy's fire more than fifty-five minutes, and that during this short time the French had 637 men killed and wounded, and the Continentals 257. "In this unsuccessful attempt," says Marshall (*Life of Washington*, vol. IV, p. 102, Philadelphia, 1805), "the loss of the French, in killed and wounded was about seven hundred men. The Continental troops lost two hundred and thirty-four men, and the Charleston Militia, who, though united with them in danger, were more fortunate, had one captain killed and six privates wounded." Irving (*Life of Washington*, vol. III, p. 522, New York, 1856), in a general way, states that the French lost in killed and wounded upwards of 600 men, and the Americans about 400. "Our troops,"

1779.　　It was difficult to persuade ourselves that we could, with about three thousand men, capture a city surrounded by entrenchments, strengthened by abattis and chevaux de frise, and defended by a garrison of four hundred and fifty men.　Nevertheless, the bravery and stubbornness exhibited by our troops, and their firmness in defeat, assure us that Savannah would have been ours if, instead of besieging, we had attacked it, sword in hand, the very day of our arrival, and if Count D'Estaing had not been deceived by the guides and officers who, despite the emphatic remonstrances of Noailles and Broves, induced him to locate his point of attack at a place where it was impracticable.

says General Moultrie, (*Memoirs, etc.*, vol. II, p. 41, New York, 1802), " remained before the lines, in this hot fire, fifty-five minutes ; the Generals, seeing no prospect of success, were constrained to order a retreat, after having 637 French and 457 Continentals killed and wounded."

" The French, killed and wounded, were rated at seven hundred men.　The American regulars suffered in proportion : two hundred and forty being killed and wounded, while the militia from Charleston, their companions in danger, lost one captain killed and six privates wounded." (*Lee's Memoirs*, vol. I, p. 109.　Philadelphia, 1812).　When driven out of the ditch and compelled to retreat, Stedman asserts (*History of the American War*, vol. II, p. 131, London, 1794), that the assailants left behind them, in killed and wounded, 637 of the French troops and 264 of the Americans.

The following are the names of some of the Continental and Militia officers killed and wounded on the 9th of October, 1779.

KILLED.　　　　　　　　Major John Jones, aid to Genl. McIntosh.
　　　　Second Regiment,　Major Motte, and Lieuts. Hume, Wickham and Bush.
　　　　Third　　"　　　Major Wise, and Lieut. Bailey.
　　　　Genl. Williamson's Brigade.　Captain Beraud.
　　　　Charlestown Regiment.　Captain Shepherd.
　　　　South Carolina Artillery.　Captain Donnom.
　　　　　　　　　　Charles Price, a volunteer, Sergt. Jasper.
WOUNDED.　Brigadier General, Count Pulaski, mortally.
　　　　Major L'Enfant, Captains Bentalou, Giles and Rogowski.
　　　Second Regiment.　Captain Roux, and Lieuts. Gray and Petrie.
　　　Third　　"　　Captain Farrar and Lieuts. Gaston and Desausure.
　　　Sixth　　"　　Captain Bowie.
　　　Virginia Levies.　Lieutenants Parker and Walker.
　　　Light Infantry.　Captain Smith of the 3d, Capts. Warren and Hogan of the 5th,
　　　　　　Lieut. Vleland of the 2d, and Lieut. Parsons of the 5th.
　　　South Carolina Militia.　Captains Davis and Treville ; Lieutenants Bonneau, Wilkie,
　　　　　　Wade and Wardel.
　　　　　　Lieutenant Edward Lloyd.　Mr. Owen.

1779. From this moment we thought only of retreat. For a long time it was unknown in the army whether this would be consummated by way of Charlestown or Thunderbolt-bluff. Several deemed it safer to retreat by land, but the manifold inconveniencies of that route, in connection with the exhaustion of our troops, fatigued by so many and great labors, determined M. D'Estaing to take his departure by sea.

To MM. de Dillon and Noailles, commanding the army, he entrusts the conduct of the retreat. The General himself was lying wounded at Thunderbolt, to which place, in obedience to his own order, he had been conveyed.[1]

[1] While it is difficult to reconcile the conflicting estimates which have been handed down to us of the forces actually engaged during the Siege of Savannah, we submit the following as the most accurate we have been able to prepare, after a careful comparison of the most reliable authorities at command.

STRENGTH OF THE FRENCH ARMY COMMANDED BY COUNT D'ESTAING.

1. *Noailles's Division*, composed of the regiments of Champagne, Auxerrois, Foix, Guadeloupe and Martinique, ... 900 men.
2. *The Division of Count D'Estaing*, composed of the regiments of Cambresis, Hainault, the Volunteers of Berges, Agenois, Gatinois, the Cape, Port au Prince, and the Artillery, ... 1,000 "
3. *Dillon's Division*, composed of the regiments of Dillon, Armagnac, and the Volunteer Grenadiers, ... 900 "
4. *The Dragoons of Condé and of Belzunce*, under the command of M. Dejean, 50 "
5. *The Volunteer Chasseurs* commanded by M. de Rouvrai, . . . 750 "
6. *The Grenadier Volunteers* and men of other regiments commanded by M. des Framais, ... 356 "
8. To these should, probably, be added the *Marines and Sailors* from the fleet, detailed for special labors, to the number of . . . . 500 "

Total, ... 4456 "

STRENGTH OF THE AMERICAN ARMY COMMANDED BY GENERAL LINCOLN.

1. CONTINENTAL TROOPS, including the Fifth regiment of South Carolina Infantry, ... 1003 men.
2. HEYWARD'S ARTILLERY, ... 65 "
3. CHARLESTON VOLUNTEERS AND MILITIA, ... 365 "
4. GENERAL WILLIAMSON'S BRIGADE, ... 212 "
5. REGIMENTS OF GEORGIA MILITIA commanded by Colonels Twiggs and Few, ... 232 "
6. CAVALRY under command of Brigadier General Count Pulaski, . 250 "

Total, ... 2,127 "

1779.

RECAPITULATION.

FRENCH TROOPS, ...	4456
AMERICAN "	2127
TOTAL STRENGTH OF THE ALLIED ARMY, ...	6,583

Anthony Stokes,* Chief Justice of the Colony of Georgia, who was in Savannah during the siege, estimates the besieging force at about 4500 French and 2500 Americans.

In the Paris Gazette of January 7, 1780, the besieging forces are enumerated as follows.

FRENCH TROOPS,

    1. *Europeans :* draughted from the regiments of Armagnac, Champagne, Auxerrois, Agenois, Gatinois, Cambresis, Haynault, Foix, Dillon, Walsh, le Cap, la Guadeloupe, la Martinique, and Port au Prince, a Detachment of the Royal Corps of Infantry of the Marine, the Volunteers of Vallelle, the Dragoons, and 156 Volunteer Grenadiers, lately raised at Cape François. }   2.979

    2. *Colored :* Volunteer Chasseurs, Mulattoes, and Negroes, newly raised at Saint Domingo, . . . }   545

AMERICAN TROOPS, ...   2,000

Total, ... 5,524

In his enclosure to Lord George Germain under date of November 5th, 1779, Governor Sir James Wright, reports the British forces within the lines of Savannah during the siege, "including Regulars, Militia, Sailors and Volunteers," as not exceeding twenty-three hundred and fifty men fit for duty. By the legend accompanying Faden's "*Plan of the Siege of Savannah,*" printed at Charing Cross on the 2d of February 1784, we are informed that the total number of English troops "including soldiers, seamen and militia garrisoning the forts, redoubts, and epaulments, and fit for duty on the 9th of October 1779," was twenty-three hundred and sixty.

"The force in Savannah under General Prevost," says the excellent historian Stedman (*History of the American War,* vol. II, p. 127, London, 1794), "did not exceed two thousand five hundred of all sorts, regulars, provincial corps, seamen, militia, and volunteers."

Dr. Ramsay, (*History of the Revolution, etc.,* vol. II, p. 40, Trenton, MDCCLXXXV,) states that "the force of the garrison was between two and three thousand, of which about one hundred and fifty were militia." General Moultrie in his *Memoirs* (vol. II, pp. 41–42,) substantially adopts this statement. "This British force," according to the estimate of Captain Hugh McCall, (*History of Georgia,* vol. II, p 270,) "consisted of two thou-sand eight hundred and fifty men, including one hundred and fifty militia, some Indians, and three hundred armed slaves." In *Rivington's Gazette* it is asserted that the entire strength of the English garrison on duty, including Regulars, Militia, Volunteers and Sailors, did not exceed 2,350 men.

---

   * *View of the Constitution of the British Colonies, etc.,* p. 116. London, MDCCLXXXIII.

1779. In the repulse of the French and Americans on the right of the English lines, the following British troops were mainly engaged.

28	dismounted Dragoons	holding the redoubts on the Ebenezer road where the brave Captain Tawse, commanding, fell.
28	Battalion men of the 60th regiment.	
54	South Carolina Loyalists	
90	of Colonel Hamilton's North Carolina Loyalists.	In the redoubt where Colonel Maitland was.
75	Militia under Captains Wallace, Tallemach and Polhill.	
74	Grenadiers of the 60th Regiment	Ordered to support the redoubt bravely charging the Allied Army when the retreat was sounded.
37	Marines.	
31	Sailors under the command of Captains Manley and Stiel.	In the Spring Battery of six guns.

417.

General Huger's attack upon the left of the British lines was repulsed by troops under command of Colonel Cruger and Major Wright.

6

1779.

Enumeration of Officers [1] *wounded the 24th of September,* 1779, *at the first Attack on the Trench, and during the Progress of the Siege of Savannah.*

	Names.	Grades and Regiments.
M M.	Amoran	Captain in Dillon's regiment.
	du Correau	idem.
	de la Mothe	" " the regiment of Champagne.
	Petiteu	2nd Lieut. " " " "
	Boisnier	Captain " " " Armagnac.
	Descures	2nd Lieut. " " " "
	Du Grés	Lieutenant " " " the Cape.
	De Cireuil	Captain " " " Gatinois.
	Vanel	Lieutenant " " " "
	Ch‍ʳ de Tourville	Lieutenant " " " "
	Grangies	2nd Lieut. " " " Port au Prince.
	Longuerice	Lieutenant " " " Martinique.
	Roch	Officer of Artillery.

Total, ...   13.

[1] The names of these officers are here given without alteration, and just as they are spelt in the manuscript.

1779.

Officers wounded the 9th of October, 1779, before Savannah.

Names.	Grades and Regiments.
M M. Count D'Estaing	General.
De Fontanges	Major General.
De Betizi	Colonel, and second in command of the regiment of Gatinois.
De Steding	Colonel of infantry.
Derneville	Aide Major of Division, mortally wounded.
Chalignon	" " " " " -
Boulan	Captain of the Grenadiers of Armagnac.
Grillere	Captain " " Regiment " "
Barris	" " " " " Augenois.
St Sauveur	Lieutenant " " " "
Chaussepred	" " " " "
Morege	2d " " " "
Chamson	Lieutenant " " " Cambresis.
Coleau	" " " " "
Boozel	Lieutenant of the Regiment of Cambresis.
Oradon	2d " " " " " Hainault.
Labarre	Lieutenant of the Dragoons of Condé.
Ouelle	Captain " " Regiment " Dillon.
Doyon	Lieutenant " " " " "
Deloy	Officer " " " " "
Ch^r de Termoi	Cadet " " " " "
Dumouries	Lieutenant " " " " the Cape.
Desombrages	" " " " " " "
Delbos	2d " " " " " " "
Desnoyers	Major " " " " Guadeloupe.
Roger	Captain " " " " "
Noyelles	Captain attached to the staff of Regiment of Guadeloupe.

1779.

Continuation of Officers wounded the 9th of October, 1779, before Savannah.

	Names.	Grades and Regiments.
M M.	D'Anglemont	Lieutenant of the chasseurs of Guadeloupe.
	De Rousson	2d " " " " " "
	Bailly de Menager	Lieutenant of the Regiment of Port au Prince, prisoner.
	Duclos	" " " Volunteer Chasseurs.

Total, ... 31.

Recapitulation of Officers killed during the Progress of the Siege.

	Names.	Grades and Regiments.
M M.	Devermont	Quarter Master of the Regiment of Gatinois.
	De Malherbe	Officer " " " " Champagne.
	Blandeau	Lieutenant " " " " Augenois.
	Justamon	" " " " " "
	Fondprose	2d " " " Volunteer Grenadiers.
	De Sencé.	Captain of Artillery.

Total, ... 6.

1779.

Officers killed on the 9th of October, 1779, the Day of the Attack.

Names.	Grades and Regiments.
M M. Brow	Major of Dillon's Regiment, Colonel of Infantry.
Balheon	Midshipman.
Destinville	Second Lieutenant of the Navy.
Molart	Lieutenant of the Regiment of Armagnac.
Stancey	2d " " " Dragoons of Condé.
Taf	Lieutenant " " Regiment of Dillon.
Guillaume	" " " Grenadiers of Guadeloupe.
De Montaign	Captain " " Chasseurs " "
Boisneuf	Lieutenant " " Regiment of Port au Prince.
Du Perron.	Captain on Staff-duty.

Total, ... 10.

Continuation of the Recapitulation.

Wounded.	Killed.
the 24th September, 1779, 10 ⎫ " 25th " . . 1 ⎪ " 4th October, . . 1 ⎬ 44. " 6th " . . 1 ⎪ " 9th " . . 31 ⎭	the 24th September, . . 4 ⎫ " 25th " . . 1 ⎪ " 26th " . . 1 ⎬ 17. " 9th October, . . 11 ⎭

Total killed and wounded, ... 61.

Recapitulation of Officers and Soldiers killed and wounded at the Siege of Savannah.

French.	Americans.
Killed, ... 377 ⎫ 821 men. Wounded, . . . 444 ⎭	Killed, ... 12 ⎫ 312 men. Wounded, . . . 300 ⎭

Total, ... 1133.

1779.   During Sunday we are occupied in dismantling our batteries, and
are undisturbed by the enemy.
Oct. 10

11th.   M. de Dillon, in acknowledgment of the humanity with which
General Prevost has treated our wounded, sends him a message that
he can remove his wife from Savannah.   Prevost delays a response,
and, when he is assured of our intention to retreat, thanks the General.

14th.   *Thursday.*   We detail two hundred and ninety-two men from the
regiments of Armagnac and Auxerrois, and from the Marines, to proceed to the enemy's left, or to the eastern side of the city, to cut off
communications with the road to Causton's creek where the army is
to embark.   These two hundred and ninety-two men are divided into
three detachments, and occupy three posts on the same line.

15th.   *Friday.*   Doubtless apprehending an attack from our new posts,
the enemy erects a work on his left.

idem.   M. de Brétigny[1] arrives from Charlestown and proposes that the
General should send there nine hundred French troops.   This the
General refuses to do.   Since the 9th of October desertions, which
ceased almost entirely after our batteries commenced playing,
increased constantly.   Every day several soldiers desert from the
different regiments.[2]

The Virginia and Georgia Militia withdraw by land, and there
remain with the army only the two American regular regiments and
Pulaski's corps.[3]

16th.   At half past four o'clock in the afternoon on Saturday, an alarm is

[1] He had been mainly instrumental in influencing Count D'Estaing to undertake this
expedition against Savannah.

[2] The fact that these desertions occurred, is distinctly corroborated by the English
accounts.

[3] The American forces under command of General Lincoln retreated by way of Ebenezer, and crossed Savannah river at Zubly's ferry.

1779. caused by musketry firing between the Americans, and the English
Oct.16 who had the boldness to come out to get water.

17th.   *Sunday.* M. de Dillon issues orders that the cooking pots and
camp utensils should be removed, and tents struck the next day at
ten o'clock. On Saturday, the 16th, the dangerously wounded are
embarked for Charlestown, and those who were suffering from slight
wounds are placed on board the various vessels of the fleet.

18th.   *Monday.* At ten o'clock in the morning, the wagons take up the
tents and camp utensils to transport them to the point of embarkation.
Sentinels are posted all around our camp to prevent desertions.

idem.   All our troops, upon which the advance guard had fallen back, are
under arms in front of the camp at eight o'clock in the evening. Our
departure is retarded in consequence of the non-return of the American
wagons. At eleven o'clock the Americans take up their line of march
to the left, and we to the right.

At one o'clock in the morning we arrive at our old camp at
Rouvrai, situated about two miles south of the eastern part of Savannah, where we bivouac for the night.

Five companies of Grenadiers and Chasseurs, guarding the trenches,
join the rear-guard at the moment of our departure. The two hundred and ninety-two men, detached on Wednesday the fourteenth of
this month, and posted to the left of the enemy where they had been
divided into three detachments and constituted the van-guard of our
army, had been relieved by the Grenadiers and the Chasseurs.

At three o'clock on Tuesday morning the retreat of the Americans,
by land, to Charlestown being regarded safe from interruption by the
enemy, all our posts are evacuated and the army begins its march for
the place of embarkation, situated on Causton's creek,[1] an arm of the
Savannah river.

---

[1] Written *Costenkrik* in the manuscript. Kincaid's landing was selected as the point
whence the troops were conveyed in small boats to the fleet.

1779.   Arriving there at five o'clock, we find our camp already established upon Causton's creek, and we commence to put our troops on board the ships.

Oct.

20th.   The greater portion of the army is embarked.

21st.   *Thursday.*   Causton's creek and all Georgia are evacuated.

24th.   *Sunday.* Departure of the *Fier Rodrigue,* with the merchant vessels under her convoy, which she escorts to the northern part of the continent.

25th.   Departure of M. de la Mothepiquet for the Leeward islands, with the ships *L'Annibal, Le Magnifique* and *Le Reflechi.*

idem.   The ships *Le Robuste, Le Sphinx, Le Diadême, Le Fendant, L'Artesien, Le Vengeur,* and *Le Dauphin Royal* receive orders from M. D'Estaing to sail for the Chesapeake, under the command of M. de Grasse.

26th.   *Tuesday* morning *Le Fendant* and *Le Diadême* weigh anchors and prepare to sail in the afternoon.   *Le Robuste* and *Le Sphinx* do the same thing.   The other ships composing the division of M. de Grasse were preparing to sail and follow him at a given signal, but they receive orders from M. D'Estaing not to depart until they had been furnished with his final instructions.

28th.   *Thursday,* at four o'clock in the afternoon, the Languedoc loses one of her cables.   She is forced to cut the other, and gets under way signalling that she cannot conform to her proper position.   *Le Tonnant* and *La Provence* encounter a similar accident a moment later, and are likewise compelled to set sail.   The north-north-west winds veering to the north-east, being very violent and exposing the fleet to constant damage, determine *Le Vengeur, L'Artesien* and *Le Dauphin Royal,* on the evening of the 26th, to make ready for sea.

7

1779.   *Saturday,* these three vessels spread their sails and depart for the
Oct. 30 Chesapeake.

31st.   *Sunday* morning a council of war is convened on board *Le Vengeur,*
at which it is decided that we will beat to the windward for four days
and wait for M. de Grasse, the division commander, and that at the
expiration of this time we will determine what further course shall be
adopted.

Nov.   *Monday,* at six o'clock in the morning, we observe some ships to the
1st.   windward which we suppose to be the vessels of M. de Grasse.   When
the day breaks we ascertain that they are our own frigates, one of
which, *La Boudeuse,* joins us and accepts the proposition we submit that
it should accompany us to the Leeward islands to which locality a
council, held the same day on board *Le Dauphin Royal,* decides that
we shall proceed immediately by the most direct course.

This morning we sighted the squadron *La Provençale* which, under
sail, was waiting for the Count D'Estaing with whom it had not yet
fallen in.   We, that is *Le Vengeur, L'Artesien, Le Dauphin Royal* and
La Boudeuse sail for the Leeward islands, steering for the Cape south-
east one quarter east.

12th.   The ship *La Boudeuse,* parts company with us and sails alone for
Grenada, her port of destination.

16th.   At eight o'clock on *Tuesday* morning we came in sight of the island
of Barbuda lying six leagues to the south.

17th.   *Wednesday,* at six o'clock in the morning, we saw Antigua distant
five leagues to the south-west.

18th.   *Thursday,* at six o'clock in the evening, we sighted Desirada, seven
leagues to the south-west.

1779.   *Friday.* M. de Retz detains a craft which we overhaul below the island of Desirada. It is a Dutch vessel, of a suspicious character, coming from Surinam.

Nov. 19th

20th.   We double Desirada at nine o'clock on Saturday evening.

21st.   *Sunday* we come in sight of Guadeloupe and Dominica, and double Mariegalanth.

Such was the termination of our enterprise against Georgia; and however sad its results may have been, it cannot be denied that it has proved productive of some advantage.

The French army has destroyed the resources which the English could have drawn from the Province for besieging Charlestown ; and, in retarding the execution of their design against that city, has afforded it an opportunity for placing itself in a posture of defense.

The city of Savannah has suffered much from the effect of our bombs and cannon balls.[1]

In consequence of the considerable captures they made, both on land and sea, our fleet and army were abundantly supplied with subsistence without cost to our King.

The English lost a ship of fifty-four guns with seven hundred thousand pounds of stores on board, a frigate, and several merchant vessels richly freighted : and were compelled to burn in the river another frigate and several vessels.[2]

[1] It is estimated that about one thousand shells and twenty carcasses were thrown into the city during the siege. By the latter several houses were consumed, among them that of Mrs. Lloyd near the church, and that of Mr. Laurie on Broughton street. Solid shot was also freely used.

[2] The following British vessels were captured by the French fleet while upon the Georgia coast: the ship *Experiment* of 50 guns, having on board Major General Garth, thirty thousand pounds sterling, and a large quantity of army stores ; the ship *Ariel* of 20 guns ; the *Myrtle,* a victualler ; the *Champion,* a store ship ; the ship *Fame ;* the ship

1779.   Finally, we destroyed Fort Tybee, where we took a piece of ordnance, the only gun the enemy had there abandoned.

Victory, richly freighted ; and several small sloops, schooners and coasting vessels laden with rice and flour.   Two privateer sloops, of 10 guns each, and three schooners were taken in Ogeechee river by Colonel White.

The ships *Rose* and *Savannah* and four transports were sunk in a narrow part of the channel of the Savannah river, below the city.   Several vessels were also sunk above the town, and a boom was stretched across the channel to prevent the French and American galleys, which passed up the north branch of the river, from rounding Hutchinson's island and attacking from that direction.

The *Rose* was sunk on the *Garden Bank*, on the 20th of September, to obstruct the river against the ascent of the French fleet.

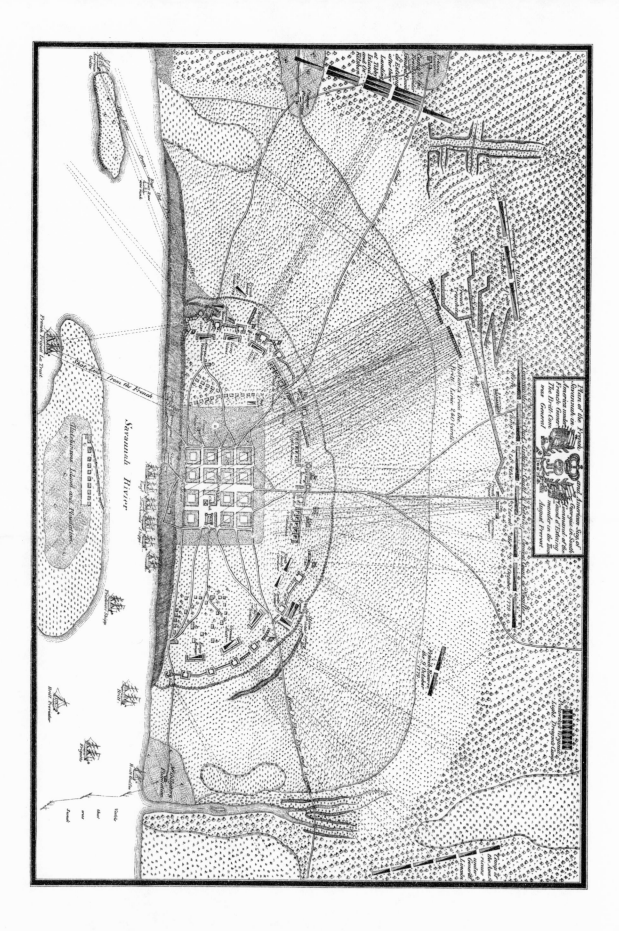

EXTRACT

FROM THE

JOURNAL OF A NAVAL OFFICER

IN THE FLEET

OF

COUNT D'ESTAING.

1782.

JOURNAL OF A NAVAL OFFICER.

SEPTEMBER, 1779.

On the second of September, because of its proximity to land of which no reconnoissance had been made, the fleet came to anchor off the coast of Florida.[1] It had passed through a violent gale which drove several of the vessels out to sea. Those which held to their anchors suffered much, some of them having been disabled by the loss of their rudders. *Le Vaillant* had hers broken, which was immediately repaired with some spare side-planks. Meanwhile, she was steered by the apparatus invented by Olivier. The General sent some frigates, under the protection of two ships, to reconnoitre the land, and ordered them to bring back some pilots. *L'Iphigénie* which, with the *Cérès*, was cruising round about the fleet, captured three prizes, the *Victory* of eighteen guns—a large ship loaded with public stores, clothing and shoes—a brigantine, and a schooner freighted with cloth.

La Chimére, l'Amazone and *le Cutter*, protected by *le Magnifique* and *le Sphinx*, returned bringing American pilots from the port of Charlestown. We all set sail immediately, navigating with caution during the day on account of the nearness of the land, and coming to anchor at night.

[1] Georgia.

8

Wednesday, the 8th of September, we made the coast of Florida.[1] That evening the fleet anchored within three leagues of the light-house,[2] at the entrance of the Savannah river in New Georgia. Of all their former possessions in this quarter of the South, the English held only Savannah and Saint Augustine.[3]

The General had been advised by M. de Bretigny, an old musketeer of the King, and at present in the service of the Americans, that the English had neglected to fortify Savannah which they had captured from the Americans in the neighborhood of Charlestown, that they were without the means of defending themselves, and had but few troops; that if he had no other special expedition in contemplation he could make this one *en passant,* and that it would occasion him but little delay. The ambition of Count D'Estaing is easily excited. Filled with the sole idea of success, he is inclined to undertake any expedition, however dangerous it may be.

He had received positive orders to return promptly to France. One cannot doubt but that the Marquis de Bouillé, cognizant of these instructions, flattered himself that, after D'Estaing's departure, he would, with the assistance of the squadron of Count de Grasse stationed at Martinique, retake Saint Lucie during the winter. There are strong reasons for believing that M. D'Estaing perceived his design; and that wishing to deprive him of the means of executing it, he determined to carry with him the choicest of the colonial troops, and, with all the naval forces to undertake expedition after expedition during the winter season.

We took possession of such small craft as attempted to escape from us along the coast. The General wished to debark his troops that night, but found that the place where he proposed to land them, and which with twenty-five men he had himself reconnoitered, was an island.[4] He then determined to place all his troops, forming a corps

[1] Should be Georgia.
[2] On the north end of Tybee island.
[3] During the revolutionary war St. Augustine constituted an important depot and *point d'appui* for the British forces in their operations against the Southern States.
[4] Great Tybee island.

of about four thousand men, including eight hundred free mulattoes taken and enlisted in the colony of Saint Domingo, on board six ships entrusted to the command of M. de la Motte-Piquet, with instructions to proceed six leagues further south to the river Saint Mary,[1] and there disembark. He was to carry with him nearly all the long boats of the vessels left at the first anchorage. The Chevalier du Rumain was ordered to enter the river with his frigate, and two store ships armed with eighteen pounder guns, and as many lighters as possible, and advance as near the city as was practicable. The frigates were engaged in guarding the various passes. *Le Sagittaire* and *le Fier Rodrigue* blockaded Port Royal.

Having made these dispositions M. D'Estaing, on the 11th of September, accompanied the six ships of M. de la Motte-Piquet, leaving the command of the fleet to the Count de Broves. He anchored that evening at the mouth of the Saint Mary[1]; and, during the night, debarked with fifteen hundred men; each soldier, in obedience to his orders, carrying provisions and water for three days.

The row-boats having accomplished this first landing[2] were desirous of returning to the ships that they might bring the remainder of the troops. Some of the long boats and canoes which, despite the bad weather, obstinately determined to leave the river in obedience to the positive instructions of the General, who knew not the difficulties which confronted them, perished. * * *

The bad weather lasted until the 18th. It was impossible to continue the disembarkation. Not even a canoe could be sent ashore. Nearly all the vessels, moored on the open coast, were forced to set sail and go far out to sea to escape destruction.

For six days Count D'Estaing remained on shore, with fifteen hundred men having only their guns, some rounds of ammunition, and three days rations, destitute of tents and baggage, exposed to a constant rain, and near enough to the enemy to apprehend an attack

[1] Vernon river.
[2] Effected at Beaulieu.

each instant.   Fortunately the enemy was ignorant of the situation of our troops.

At last the weather permitted us to finish the debarkation; and Count D'Estaing, without losing a moment, advanced upon the enemy whom he found entrenched below the city of Savannah. With the few troops under his command he could not attack with hope of success. Many have thought he should, under the circumstances, have then reëmbarked. It is certain, had he done so, he would have followed a wiser plan, for his entire fleet was lying exposed upon the coast. But this is judgment after event. M. D'Estaing could rely on the coöperation of the Americans. Major General Prevost seemed inclined to surrender. In a conference he announced that he would, to save his honor, make an apparent defense; but Colonel Meklen[1] who with seven hundred men, threw himself into the place by way of Saint Augustine creek,[2] changed all at once these pacific dispositions.

Count D'Estaing opened a trench at half musket range of the English entrenchment, with a fearlessness characteristic of his valor. Cannons, mortars, bombs and the necessary munitions of war were wanting. The fleet, which was to supply these, was moored six leagues from Savannah.[3] During the month of September the weather was constantly unpropitious. Often for five and six consecutive days we were unable to send our row-boats to sea, and the ships were compelled to continue under sail for fear of being driven upon the coast. Count D'Estaing displayed great courage in exposing so considerable a fleet, moored on the high seas, for two months, to the danger of shipwreck upon the coast from the south-east winds. It was not until Monday, the fourth of October, that the cannons and mortars were in position and ready to open fire.

During this period the ships had not been inactive. On the eleventh of September, after a protracted engagement, *l'Amazon* captured the frigate *Ariel* of twenty guns. The Chevalier du Rumain with *la Bricole*

1 Maitland.
2 *Wall's cut*, and the *Savannah river.*
3 Spelt in the narrative *Savanah.*

and *la Truite* had advanced up the river and forced the English frigate *Rose* and several merchant vessels to burn themselves. He also took possession of a ship laden with timber for masts. Taking advantage of high water he advanced each tide, being engaged in a steady conflict with the English galleys which harrassed him night and day to such a degree that the captains of the two American galleys who were acting in concert with him grew weary of the continuous fight. One of them had his galley secretly scuttled by a sailor to whom he promised a hundred half crowns if he would sink it to the bottom. Coming to a knowledge of this fact, the Chevalier du Rumain himself assumed command of the vessel. Being unable to advance any further with his frigate, on account of the shallowness of the water, he anchored *la Truite,* which drew less water than his frigate, within cannon shot of the English entrenchments and of the city, and fired day and night upon the camp.

On the 27th of September the Chevalier de Cöetendo, commanding *le Lively,* by a ruse and in genuine corsair style, captured two large ships, one freighted with provisions, and the other with anchors and cables, which reported that they were under the escort of the ship *Experiment* which was accompanying a convoy to Savannah, and from which they had been separated by a gale. Upon receipt of this intelligence three of our ships were detached to cruise off Port Royal.

On the 24th the frigate *la Cérès* made herself master of a large ship loaded with provisions, under the escort of the *Experiment.* This prize and those which preceded it could not have been more seasonable. The navy was beginning to need provisions and was obliged to economize in everything, particularly in water which was doled out in a cruel way even to the sick. Neglect had occurred in this important particular; no use having been made of the American boats which had come to us, suitable for the navigation of the river, and for which the king was at no charge.

The navy is suffering everything, anchored on an open coast and liable to be driven ashore by the south-east winds. Happily we have had only gusts of wind from the north-east which injured seven of our ships in their rudders. Several have lost all their anchors, and most of them have been greatly endamaged in their rigging. The scurvy rages with such severity that we throw into the sea, each day, thirty-five men.

We have no kind of refreshments to give the sick; not even *tisanne*, by reason of the lack of water. There was no way of alleviating the misery of our poor sailors who, wanting coats, destitute of linen, without shoes, and absolutely naked, had nothing to eat except salt provisions which made them die of thirst. The bread which we possessed, having been two years in store, was so much decayed and worm eaten, and was so disagreeable to the taste, that even the domestic animals on board would not eat it. Even this had to be distributed in scanty rations for fear that the supply would utterly fail. Behold a part of the frightful picture of the cruel and miserable condition of our crews during the continuance of the Siege of Savannah, upon which the Count D'Estaing was so intent that he appeared to have entirely forgotten his vessels. The few sailors who were in condition to work the ships, were weak, of a livid color, with the marks of death painted on their faces, and could not be viewed without compassion. During the night occurring between the 24th and the 25th of September, our vessels in cruising gave an alarm to the fleet by coming to anchor suddenly in our midst when we were not on the look out for them.

The reason for this haste proved very agreeable to us in our deplorable situation. They brought intelligence of the capture of the *Experiment*, a ship of fifty guns, by *le Sagittaire* which fell in with her off Port Royal, wholly dismasted and incapable of offering any resistance. This vessel was conveying officers for the army of Savannah. She carried Major General Garth who was coming to relieve General Prevost. What was of greater value, however, was the pay for the army at Savannah, six hundred and sixty thousand silver livres of France. This news afforded us the greatest pleasure. We learned from the prisoners, taken on this ship, that she had sailed from New York in convoy with three thousand troops for Savannah, escorted by three ships of the line. M. de Broves, accompanied by four ships, cruised incessantly to intercept them. This convoy was undoubtedly warned of its danger, as it never made its appearance.

Let us return to the siege. On the 23rd of September the English made a sortie upon our working parties. M. de Rouvré who commanded the trench, having under him Lieutenant Colonel M. O'Dune, repulsed them vigorously. M. O'Dune was drunk. His natural courage and the excitement caused by the wine carried him beyond the proper limits which had been prescribed. His indiscreet impetuosity cost us one hundred and fifty men placed *hors de combat*, of whom forty were killed, struck down in their retreat by the enemy's artillery. To replace this loss the General ordered up four hundred marines from the fleet, under the command of their own officers. This weakened the fleet still more. From that time it was in no condition to fight, even if an occasion had presented itself and Biron[1] had made his appearance. The Lieutenant of the navy who commanded this corps of four hundred men, took rank in the trenches as a superior officer, and commanded in his turn.

Monday, the 4th of October, our cannon and mortar batteries commenced to fire. Our cannon produced no effect upon the enemy's entrenchments constructed of sand and with sloping glacis. The balls made no holes, but simply buried themselves. Our bombs succeeded a little better. The General caused carcasses, filled with turpentine, to be thrown into the city, which several times set it on fire. These harrassed the English who had their wives and children shut in, exposed to all the horrors of the siege. The Chevalier du Rumain remained upon the side towards the sea, with two galleys and *la Truite*, whose stray shots, passing over the camp, traversed the streets of the city.

The English attempted to encamp their women and children on a small island.[2] The Chevalier du Rumain made a descent there at the same time and compelled them to return to the city. Seeing no other alternative, they addressed themselves to Count D'Estaing, praying permission to send out their women and children. This request he refused because, if granted, there was likelihood of the prolongation of

[1] The English Admiral, Lord Byron.
[2] Hutchinson's island.

the siege of which he began to grow weary. Many women however, left the city and presented themselves of their own accord at the French camp. It was necessary for us to take good care of them as they were unwilling to return. General Prevost, whose generosity and humanity towards French prisoners have never been denied, had given them tokens of attention and goodness which could scarcely have been expected from an enemy. This conduct on his part was, without doubt, due in great measure to his wife, born French. It was jestingly remarked by a member of parliament that our gallantry could not be denied even in our manner of making war, and that the prettiest woman of the city came to test the effect of our bombs.

The desperate and pitiable condition of our fleet, deprived of two thirds of its equipment and anchored in a position where, by the admission of the prisoners, an English squadron had never dared to remain for eight hours even in the most beautiful weather, decided Count D'Estaing — seeing that his cannon could effect no practicable breach — to make a sudden assault.

The enemy had not less than four thousand men within their entrenchments, including some militia upon whom they could rely.[1] In all, M. D'Estaing had not three thousand troops upon whom he could count, and about eighteen hundred Americans, among whom was a small number of regulars commanded by Pulaski, a Pole.

Orders were issued for the troops to be in readiness to march to the assault upon the entrenchments at four o'clock in the morning of the 9th of October. In accordance with the instructions given by M. D'Estaing, arrangements were made during the night by M. de Fontanges, Major General of the army and Colonel of the Volunteers of the Cape. He has been generally blamed for having, at two o'clock in the morning, and at the moment of marching, divided and subdivided the companies of Grenadiers, placing over them officers, strangers to the corps, and with whom they had no personal acquaintance. Major Brown of Dillon's regiment, in representing the consequences, condemned

---

[1] An over estimate, as we have already seen.

the general order of attack. His advice was not taken. The result proved that he was correct, but he himself lost his life on this occasion. M. D'Estaing caused a false attack to be made upon the entrenchments on our right, near a strong battery; at the same time he led the assault upon our left, having to pass through a morass in which our soldiers mired to their knees, at the end of which was an abattis of trees, most difficult to pass through, and swept by the enemy's artillery. It was evident beyond a doubt — and we were advised of the fact soon afterwards — that the enemy had been informed by an American[1] of all our dispositions and of the hour of the attack. We may add to this statement the further circumstance that the British troops had large white cockades and shirts over their coats, which were precisely the prescribed marks by which we were to recognize each other during the conflict.

The General[2] encountered the fire of the enemy's artillery charged with grape-shot, which cut his column to the centre. Perceiving that his column was recoiling, the General passed to its head and, with his bravest men, marched in advance up to the abatis. He was followed by only three or four hundred Grenadiers and many officers. This little troop, led by the General, rushed up to the entrenchments and effected a lodgment in the ditch in such a position that the English could not bring their guns to bear upon us. Here a hand to hand conflict ensued. These brave men were not seconded. The rest of the column, entangled in the swamp, was mowed down by the enemy's artillery, in the face of which it could not advance.

In traversing the abattis, through which he had forced his way with great difficulty, the General received two severe wounds. Nevertheless, he still retained strength and courage sufficient to mount his horse and in person order a retreat. It was in retiring that these brave Grenadiers, who had penetrated even into the ditch, were cut to pieces by the grape-shot from the artillery of the English, who fired packets of

[1] Sergeant Major Curry.
[2] Count D'Estaing.

9

scrap-iron, the blades of knives and scissors, and even chains five and six feet long. The Chevalier du Rumain attempted to make a demonstration with his galleys in the direction of the river; but, encountering insurmountable difficulties, accomplished nothing.

Our loss was considerable. By the returns rendered, six hundred and eighty men had been put *hors de combat;* of whom sixty-four were officers. Among the latter twenty-two were either killed in action or died shortly thereafter.

Our troops, without exception, extolled the bravery of the American Regulars commanded by Pulaski. With astonishing gallantry they returned twice to the assault, planted their flags upon the parapet of the entrenchments, and rallied in good order after having lost their chief, wounded to the death. As for the militia, they fled in a cowardly manner in the woods even before the action commenced. During the cessation of hostilities which ensued, Colonel Meklen[1] absolutely wished to count our dead and wounded before extending to them any relief. The loss sustained by the English was very small. They had only fifteen men killed. This is not remarkable, when we consider the manner in which they were entrenched.

The General with his two wounds, that in the leg being very serious, would not suffer himself to be carried. He rode on horseback to the village of Thunderbolt[2] in company with Major General de Fontanges, who had received a gun-shot wound through the body. Here the General remained until his return to his ship on Monday the 18th of October, having given orders for the retreat which was accomplished the same evening, under the direction of M. de Dillon, in the long-boats and barges from the fleet, and without interruption by the enemy. Two days previously the Americans had retired, taking up their line of march for Charlestown.

When the fleet was informed of the repulse of our army in the assault of the 9th, in addition to all our distresses *le Magnifique* sprung a leak and we were unable to free her from water with all the ship's

[1] Maitland.
[2] Spelt *Thunderbloc* in the Journal.

pumps which were worked day and night without intermission. We were compelled to stay her against a merchant vessel while we dispatched to land our row-boats which constituted our only means for procuring succor.

Our situation had become terrible and disheartening. We were obliged to receive on board many wounded, with no refreshments to offer them, without even linen with which to dress their wounds, and were forced to leave as quickly as possible, for a thousand reasons, the least of which was imperative, with no point of relief nearer than the Chesapeake, one hundred and fifty leagues away, and with winds nearly always contrary.

Moreover, the General desired at once to take his final departure from Savannah for France, with his squadron of Provence. Water, consequently, was necessary. We at length found the means of procuring it from the river at low tide, brackish as it was. Necessity, the mother of industry, made us accomplish in four days what we had not for two months ventured to attempt.

The Count de Grasse, with his squadron of eight vessels carrying our wounded and those afflicted with the scurvy, was dispatched for the Chesapeake. Thence he was to sail for the Windward islands. M. de la Motte-Piquet with three ships, including *le Maynifique* in an unseaworthy condition, was commissioned to reconduct to the Cape what remained of the troops which had been drawn from that colony. The frigates were ordered to carry to Grenada and Saint Vincent the detachments of Hainault and Foix. The Chevalier du Rumain, with his frigate and two armed store-ships, had Charlestown as his point of destination. It is believed that he was charged with the defense of that place in case of an attack.

The ships of Provence were manned for navigation with all the prisoners, who were forced to work in view of present necessity. Just as the General had matured all his plans a wind-storm arose — unfortunate circumstance which can happen only at sea — in consequence of which he was compelled to set sail without issuing the orders requisite for carrying out the arrangements he had made.   *   *   *

The wind storm which forced the General to set sail on the 28th of October ceased on the 30th; and on the 31st the Count de Broves convened the captains and consulted as to what course should be adopted in case M. D'Estaing did not again make his appearance. Upon this supposition, and without taking into consideration the time which might be necessary for him to rejoin us, it was unanimously resolved that we should set sail that very evening, taking sea-room some leagues to the windward, and that after cruising several days, waiting for the General, should he not appear, we would steer for France; M. D'Estaing having intimated his desire to return thither as quickly as possible.

I permit myself to observe, in this connection, that the condition of the weather giving no occasion for alarm and being even favorable to M. D'Estaing's rejoining us, it was necessary that we should at least allow him time to do so, and hold ourselves in readiness to sail upon the first appearance of a storm. It seemed probable that M. D'Estaing lacked anchors, having let go the only two which he had, in the hope that they would take firm hold and prevent him from being forced to sea. It was therefore more than likely that he would return to take up the smaller of these anchors, even if he did not come back to finish giving his orders. The two days spent in waiting for him, while we were obeying his instructions, were made profitable to the public service in that they were employed in raising the anchors of the ships which had been compelled to cut them.

On the 31st M. de Broves got under way with a portion of his ships, and came to anchor half a league to the windward of his first anchorage. The next day the others set sail to appear here no more, leaving *l'Ariel*, laden with mulattoes, without destination. M. du Rumain was still in the river, not having received his orders. The frigates, under the command of M. de Marigny, departed for Grenada.

The first night we were under way, with most beautiful weather, *le Marseillois* and *le Zélé* separated themselves from us and steered together for France. *Le Tonnant* and *la Provence* were already absent, having been obliged to get under way four hours after *le Languedoc*. M. de Broves, having cruised four and twenty hours only, at ten o'clock in the morning of the 2d of November sailed away with seven vessels, including the *Experiment* and the frigate *l'Amazone*. Thus is the fleet, by reason of its forced separation from the General, divided and subdivided into so many parts that, without the intervention of a miracle, it appears quite impossible that each vessel will arrive safely at her destination.

The enterprise against Savannah seemed to cost France dear when we consider the condition of affairs it brought about. The Count D'Estaing was all the more inexcusable because he exposed our colonies to a similar expedition ; leaving the Windward islands without protection and abandoned to themselves, thus affording the English, strong in this quarter, an opportunity, had they so wished, at any time within three months of retaking them, perhaps of recapturing Saint Vincent and even Grenada — where they would have enjoyed excellent winter harbor—and of attacking Martinique enfeebled by having her troops continually withdrawn to participate in these expeditions. Why, after the battle of Grenada, did he desire to remain, instead of returning to France as an escort to the convoy, in obedience to orders from the Court, leaving Count de Grasse in the Windward islands with his eight vessels to protect them and confirm the conquests he had come to make ?

Covetous of glory, excited by his successes, and easily seduced by an invitation from the sieur de Bretigny who made him believe that the conquest of Savannah was an easy matter, Count D'Estaing was unable to resist a desire, rising superior to the hazard, to attempt to add new triumphs to those which he had already achieved.

If zeal, activity, eagerness, and ambition to accomplish great deeds are worthy of recompense, never will France be able sufficiently to acknowledge her obligations to Count D'Estaing. With much intelligence, he possesses the enthusiasm and the fire of a man twenty years of age. Enterprising, bold even to temerity, all things appear possible to him. He fancies no representations which bring home to him a knowledge of difficulties. Whoever dares to describe them as formidable, is illy received. He wishes every one to view and think of his plans as he does. The sailors believe him inhuman. Many died upbraiding him with their misery, and unwilling to pardon him; but this is a reproach incident to his austere mode of life, because he is cruel to himself. We have seen him sick and attacked with scurvy, never desiring to make use of any remedies, working night and day, sleeping only an hour after dinner, his head resting upon his hands, sometimes lying down, but without undressing.

Thus have we observed Count D'Estaing during this campaign. There is not a man in his fleet who would believe that he has endured all the fatigue which he has undergone. When I am now asked if he is a good general, it is difficult for me to respond to this inquiry. He committed much to chance and played largely the game of hazard. But that he was energetic, adventurous almost to rashness, indefatigable in his enterprises which he conducted with an ardor of which had we not followed him we could have formed no conception, and that to all this be added much intellect, and a temper which imparted great austerity to his character, we are forced to admit.

INDEX.